# Pitch: Drafts 77–95

The long poem project of Rachel Blau DuPlessis, begun in 1986, is collected here, in *Pitch: Drafts 77–95* (2010), in *Torques: Drafts 58–76* (2007), in *Drafts 39–57, Pledge, with Draft unnumbered: Précis* (2004), all from Salt Publishing, as well as in *Drafts 1–38, Toll* (Wesleyan U.P., 2001). *The Collage Poems of Drafts* is forthcoming from Salt at the end of 2010. In 2006, two books of innovative essays by DuPlessis were published: *Blue Studios: Poetry and Its Cultural Work* on gender and poetics, and a reprint of *The Pink Guitar: Writing as Feminist Practice*, both from University of Alabama Press. Her other critical writing includes *Genders, Races, and Religious Cultures in Modern American Poetry, 1908–1934* (Cambridge University Press, 2001); she also edited *The Selected Letters of George Oppen* (1990). In 2002 she was awarded a Pew Fellowship in the Arts and the Roy Harvey Pearce/Archive for New Poetry Prize; in 2007, a residency for poetry at Bellagio; and in 2008–09, an appointment to the National Humanities Center in North Carolina. Her websites are http://wings.buffalo.edu/epc/authors /duplessis and http://rachelblauduplessis.com

# Books, chapbooks, edited books and editions by Rachel Blau DuPlessis

*Purple Passages: Patriarchal Poetry and its Ends.* forthcoming.

*The Collage Poems of Drafts.* London: Salt Publishing, 2010.

*Pitch: Drafts 77–95.* London: Salt Publishing, 2010.

*Torques: Drafts 58–76.* Cambridge: Salt Publishing, 2007.

*The Feminist Memoir Project: Voices from Women's Liberation.* New Brunswick: Rutgers University Press, 2007. Anthology co-edited with Ann Snitow. Reprint of the 1998 book, with a new preface.

*The Pink Guitar: Writing as Feminist Practice.* Tuscaloosa: University of Alabama Press, 2006. Reprint of the 1990 book.

*Blue Studios: Poetry and Its Cultural Work.* Tuscaloosa: University of Alabama Press, 2006.

*DRAFTS. Drafts 39–57, Pledge with Draft, Unnumbered: Précis.* Cambridge, England: Salt Publishing, 2004.

*Draft, unnumbered: Précis.* Vancouver: Nomados, 2003.

*Drafts 1–38, Toll.* Middletown, CT: Wesleyan University Press, 2001.

*Genders, Races, and Religious Cultures in Modern American Poetry, 1908–1934.* Cambridge, England: Cambridge University Press, 2001.

*The Objectivist Nexus: Essays in Cultural Poetics.* Tuscaloosa: The University of Alabama Press. Anthology co-edited with Peter Quartermain, 1999.

*The Feminist Memoir Project: Voices from Women's Liberation.* New York: Three Rivers/ Crown Publishing Group, 1998. Anthology co-edited with Ann Snitow.

*Renga: Draft 32.* Philadelphia: Beautiful Swimmer Press, 1998.

*Drafts 15–XXX, The Fold.* Elmwood, CT: Potes & Poets Press, 1997.

*Essais: Quatre Poèmes.* Traduction collective, Royaumont, revue et complétée par Jean-Paul Auxeméry. Bar-le-Duc, France: Un Bureau sur l'Atlantique, Editions Créaphis, 1996.

*Draft X: Letters.* Philadelphia: Singing Horse Press, 1991.

*Drafts 3–14.* Elmwood, CT.: Potes & Poets Press, 1991.

*The Pink Guitar: Writing as Feminist Practice.* New York: Routledge, 1990.

*Signets: Reading H.D.* Madison: University of Wisconsin Press. Anthology co-edited with Susan Stanford Friedman, 1990.

*The Selected Letters of George Oppen.* Rachel Blau DuPlessis, ed. Durham, N.C.: Duke University Press, 1990.

*Tabula Rosa.* Elmwood, CT: Potes & Poets Press, 1987.

*H.D.: The Career of that Struggle.* London: Harvester and Bloomington: Indiana University Press, 1986.

*Writing Beyond the Ending: Narrative Strategies of Twentieth-Century Women Writers.* Bloomington: Indiana University Press, 1985.

*Gypsy/Moth.* Oakland, CA: Coincidence Press, 1984.

*Wells.* New York: Montemora Editions, 1980. Selected for the Duration Press Online Out of Print Book Archives, 1999. http://www.durationpress.com

# Pitch

## Drafts 77–95

## Rachel Blau DuPlessis

London

PUBLISHED BY SALT PUBLISHING
Fourth Floor, 2 Tavistock Place, Bloomsbury, London WC1H 9RA United Kingdom

Salt Publishing 2010

Printed and bound in the United States by Lightning Source UK Inc

Typeset in Swift 9.5 / 13

ISBN 978 1 84471 747 7 paperback

1 3 5 7 9 8 6 4 2

*to Koré Simone DuPlessis*

# Contents

# Acknowledgements

Drafts 77–95, with acknowledgment to all the editors listed.

Draft 77: Pitch Content. In *The i.e. Reader*. Michael Ball, ed. Baltimore: Narrow House, 2009.

Draft 78: Buzz Track. *Integral(le)s*, ed Andrew Fitch, 2009. The first two Codas were published by the Poetry Collection, SUNY-Buffalo Library as their Holiday Broadside, 2008. With thanks to Mike Basinski and James Maynard.

Draft 79: Mass Observation. *Xcp: Cross-cultural Poetics* 18 (2007), Mark Nowak, ed.

Draft 80: Envoi. *Veer Off*. Stephen Mooney, ed. (October 2008): 82–84.

Draft 81: Gap. *BlackBox Manifold* (Summer 2009). Alex Houen and Adam Piette, eds. http://www.manifold.group.shef.ac.uk/

Draft 82: Hinge. *Conjunctions* 50 (May 2008), Bradford Morrow, ed.

Draft 83: Listings. *Alligatorzine* (November 2007). Number 50. Kurt Devrese, ed. http://www.alligatorzine.be/pages/zine.html

Draft 84: Juncture. *Salt Magazine*. John Kinsella., ed. 2009.

Draft 85: Hard Copy. *Web Conjunctions* (September 2007). Bradford Morrow, ed. http://www.conjunctions.com/webcon/duplessis07.htm This poem was written in largest measure during a residency at Bellagio, with many thanks to the Rockefeller Foundation.

Draft 86: Scarpbook. Love, War & Last Things. Michele Leggott, ed. After being written, the poem was "set" in a digital and visual format by Brian Flaherty. I am grateful to Leggott and to her colleagues for the invitation to participate in this project. www.nzepc.auckland.ac. nz / features/florence.asp

Draft 87: Trace Elements. *Verse* 26, nos. 1–3 (2009). Brian Henry and Andrew Zawacki eds.: 309–342. With great thanks to the Poetics of the Trace conference, held at Monash University, Melbourne, Australia in July 2008.

Draft 88: X-Posting. *Jacket Magazine* 35. December 2007–2008. John Tranter, ed. http://jacketmagazine.com/35/duplessis-draft88.shtml

Draft 89: Interrogation. *Jacket Magazine* 35. December 2007–2008. John Tranter, ed. http://jacketmagazine.com/35/duplessis-draft 89.shtml

Draft XC: Excess. *Talisman*. Ed Forster and Joe Donahue, eds.

Draft 92: Translocation. *EOAGH* 5, ed. Tim Peterson, ed

Draft 94: Mail Art. *Jacket Magazine* 37, http://jacketmagazine.com /37/ma38.shtml With many thanks to the Bellagio Foundation, where this work was begun, and to Phillip Barron, National Humanities Center, who helped definitively with the web version.

Draft 95: Erg. Forthcoming from *The Denver Quarterly*.

# Grid of Drafts

# Draft 77: Pitch Content

> *"It wants to write. It wants me to
> write it . . ."*

A
first page empty, blank and null.
The table clear.
Begin. But how? as Empty? Full?
And where?

If "letters took on
. . . the shape of great mountains"
the Book
or B
      would show itself as wall,
      writing scribbled on off-cuts,
      marks smuggled into cracks,
          opening, penetration, fold, hinge;
          leave something, leave anything.
          A dot, a smudge, a scrap.

But something unfathomable
does not accede.
      Forget the glyph;
      flood the letter.
This fell into itself, beyond.
Beyond theater
beyond matter.
      It vibrates
      its solidified darkness.
One arc of oscillation
marks ten million years.

To comprehend is null, is nil.
        And "Y" has had its term.
                (Indeed.)

And figure "N" (that one you
        might have thought was firm)
                dissolves into impacted resonance.

Thus can consider it all
        (all it)
                As catches, caches
Caught where the incalculable tolls.

This fecund generation from
an iterated
Sound, from
that Unseeable micro-tonal
swathe, this groan
Beyond Negative, beyond Positive
cannot have a Verb,
no verb that's conjugate, or known.

        A dirtied ragged
        Unhearable hum
        Beyond beyond
        Understudies from.

All waves and sounded shimmers thus
spread everywhere
across such plausible-implausible time or shape
become themselves unfathomable.
The centerpiece is dark.

The edges darker.
Or the reverse.

Therefore: finality.
　　No meaning, really.
No more to say, no more be said.
　　And so, farewell.


　．


No, stay!

　　　Given that pitch content can shape out
　　　from the rumble harmonics
　　　of this abyssal resonance,
　　　Given that the intricate Plenitude
　　　of massed overtones,
　　　"timbral Extravagance,"
　　　Cross-eyed Interface,
　　　and dream Concussion
　　　do enflame,

　　　You need begin again.

　　　Hudson Seine Sorge Crum
　　　Schuylkill Tevere Niccone,
　　　Ten million years—can call it
　　　Normalized Quondam Vertigo.

　　　　　All discussable!
　　　　　(We cannot not think so.)

Farewell, Hello.
Say yes; say no;
The Y, the N, It's All, or Here,
or One, or Not;
it is the It
of impercipient vibrato—
illimitable sound-move in unthinkable space.

That drone between the swing
is Everything:
the here that's resonant,
a there that's unrecoverable,
whatever's happened and
sideshadows of event,
whatever did not,

the whole and the lost, the lost and the rent
in this ferocious, implacable vibration
excite "a near-traumatic astonishment."

JANUARY 2006–SEPTEMBER 2008

# Draft 78: Buzz Track

In the urban scavenger tradition
in the beaded angel tradition,
a chatter, a riddle and
completely itiomatic, yes

in the pluck dark in-purp, pupa-pack
tradition of stuffed grape leaves making
butterflies, joke (but more),
all pica pica magpie, all blowing
treble shimmer and naked splendor,
      a piping switt-witt-witt, and ah-I in alarm,
rouge
      splashing water
                  and unparsable thoughts:
                        all are present, here.

Each single word, each labile letter
opens a mini-world
from particular presence and long implication.
Then they and we, you and I, he, she, and it
pronominal volunteers
reflect and refract
infinitudes of twirls and networks.

There are little sounds
swung hinged
in the woods;
lucid rrrrr-
rambles of high pitched notes
whistle a true twsee-ee
warble a tune wow.

The melody "children go where I"
a minute later
"send thee"
then after beat,
the off bleat
blehhh
("raspberry")

Honey skep

Overlip.

S/one stalks those sprechstimme blues.
Yeah, it's noise that stays noise, *nous* saying news,
with a go and a blow and a ho-T-ho
and a We and a twee and a twisted three
cawing heh-heh-heh
and hoo-poo-poo,
and KUK oo,
random biddyings
swoop to the road, lope, this torsion and pip
that loop around the fitted middle of "home."

Birddwingg, and the creamy cloud of sky.
High scintillation and undulate Uncanny,
"low, far-carrying, ringing laugh"
charged with Aspect-variant luminosity.

Given such trails of bricolage and randomness, such
sieve passages and catch obituaries,
*it* articulates best as tru-it, pipp-it, it-it.
It's Multiple exposure of the bright debris.

Similarly
*yiou* and *thwe* and *wey* and *hheer*
emerge on the pronoun grid
as what we always knew but never before said.

And on those premises, Thwe and Tsee-tsee
double up, combine,
it is the strangest thing—
enormous, chryselephantine
in a precious intention:

our pronouns sound of birds.
To substitute for nouns, it's birds.
Hwaet?
Here's the pitch—
Here's argument:

We need more pronouns.

How else to link us, who we really are:

The sound of thwe or yiou will do.

Pronouns, very birds.

We veery truly.

Full spectrum of persons,

but webbed in feathers.

Cheep sharp, chirp flat,

So-called "me" as it-it-it.

Real pronouns at the merge

of boundary

in such a way as this entanglement

manifests ever more attractive labyrinths

in which glistening relations link-link.

Crows chase off the honey buzzard,

buzzard stalks the crows. It's no picnic.

But that's what's here. Try to get it.

Me-she. Me-it.

Beak beak.


CODA

"Rich, mellow, melodious warble,
Fluted notes
Often with weak, chuckled ending."

A moving thing, the
I of the blackbird.

Blackbird whistle (Y) i-o-u
descending a sequence called letters
solo concerto without orchestra

leaves
on the
ayre
ebb
esque?


OTHER CODAS

A) Every hairy bit of matter and its sound,
noise shed like light upon the littler
noises darkening below syntax,
such hubbub under the sidereal
such ferny ferns and grassy grass and rosy rose
reveal a chiaroscuro push-pull. Call it hope.
This seems somewhat sentimental?
But if it continues to be true

        we'll have lucked
        totally out.


B) The air being
polyphonous
bliss, the world
being criss-crosst
spectra of intercut waves, and that
shimmery stuff

being the high-protein hairgrass of          really
precarious apprenticeships,                     it's—
we could try to be content                        what?
grazing on this                                         feeling again that
fine and implacable abyss.                     it's irresistible.


JULY 2006; JANUARY–JULY 2007; JUNE 2008

# Draft 79: Mass Observation

1. Any over-boiled egg presents a grey-green halo on its
    hardened yolk.
    2. Who then said aura is lost?

3. The sadness comes with the territory.
        4. The all of it—the gesture, the space,

   the boomerang throw,
            the reflection a hundred times, things never seen but
            felt —

5. Plan: Rip it all in half and half again. 6. Did this help?
        7. Sign Testing is in Progress. Watch for new detours.

8. At least with radar there is a landing beam
        and someone, even in the fog, can follow it.

9. Who could credit such a stalemate? Such numbness?
        10. A Gridlock of Possessions impedes the richer "of."

11. Former agreements can no longer be evoked.
        12. This poem is written in blind verse. In "black verse."

13. Landscape stinks of the historical but mainly impalpably.
        14. Except for sheep. The car is stuck in them. Can't
        move

   for just a moment.
        15. Plan: write only epistles.

16. What is the name of that funny little island where there
        are no taxes and U.S. businesses use it to make things?

17. It seems there *is* no post-war.
    Post-war is war?

18. These details are too real; there is nothing to be charmed by,
    none of the reverberating distance of art.

19. If you are surprised.
    20. "We do this by taking a long-term approach."

21. A woman scavenged food, quick-checks its general viability.
    22. Dream: the top of our house a ruin.

23. Catalogue has to do, to do this.
    24. Plan: a nekuia based on digression.

25. Every morning an account of crimes is delivered, to recycle
    tomorrow.
    26. This piece of fruit tastes like absolutely nothing.

27. We try not to drink industrial waste.
    28. Is all our decisiveness really relevant?

29. This return receipt acknowledges only that the message
    was displayed on the recipient's machine.

30. There is no guarantee that the content
    has been read or understood.

31. Plan: to write propaganda. 32. Not.
    33. Is the emphasis on luck, choice or

on horrors, the harrowing and hapless Helplessness?
34. This train is hopelessly delayed.

35. Many are the limens one cannot go back on,
like when the last of a species dies of old age.

36. Sometimes words are chosen from the newspapers;
sometimes one doesn't know exactly what to chose.

37. Yet if enough notations and idioms are collected,
visibility will increase. 38. And then what? Was it just to
record?

Just to make a record? Just to make some mark?
39. To say what life was like "then" is not totally shabby.

40. To account for rooms, failures, devastation,
plans (workable and not), the modes of folding and
caring

makes a kind of goal. 41. Is it goal enough?
42. "This is going to be a by-the-numbers, by-the-book
investigation."

43. Technique is just a tool.
44. Sleepers under the station overhang pee by the
access stairs.

45. Even a documentary only stretches so far.
46. Although, certainly, technique is not neutral.

47. Glass smash on the street, a flattened plastic bottle: of this.
      48. Low production values—automatically more credible?

49. He "earned $69.7 million—$190,000 a day—in 2005."
      50. Living under a smash and grab government.

51. To listen for anything but pure voracity is inaccurate.
      52. "You can have it all (without the fat & calories)."

53. Didn't he write "Esthétique do Mal"?
      54. It takes the advice of an investment professional

to put that information into context.
      55. "There will be much to avoid in this poem."

56. Toll plaza.
      57. Sovegna vos.

58. It was civic and optimistic when it first opened.
      59. "I'd like the record to show ... "

60. Failed development paradigm.
      61. The political economy of *Gelassenheit* was what?

62. Multiple exposure of the bright debris.
      63. Memorably strange and particular details.

64. Seen from the air, "We" are just another "Them."
      65. Off-curb dream jerk made him fall awake.

66. The atmosphere: suspicion, distrust, crumbling
      hegemony, major crisis magnetizing chronic crises.

67. Is it enough to say all this again?
  68. And incredible rage, our keepers incompetent,

incontinent. Our shunters derisory, our stewards—
  predators.  69. Is there joy yet

at the discovery? Is there hope?
  70. Just isolating this gives information.

71. But there is also the penetrating sense
  of running out of time.

72. Did these years have to happen the way they did?
  The damage of days in the general seeking and shattering?

73. "There is little public outcry about mistaken policies."
  74. I spent three of the past four nights poisoning myself
    with dread.

75. So I am a demonstrative particle. 76. And it's "not just a car,
  but a 5-passenger sanctuary from the worst the elements
    can throw at you."

77. Buy more, buy this, buy it. Buy now.
  78. Call this Collateral Wreckage.

79. Stamped "Embargo: government publication; not to be
  released."
  But the bureaucrats were cool with that.

80. Sleep two more hours to erase such dreams.
  81. Plan: there is none.

82. "The elements" is a code word.
      83. Everything depends on maintaining an enemy at its
          peak.

84. She said "no need to repeat the news."
      But it's all news all the time, what I have/ what this has
          said,

every which word and every way of this.
      85. They organize even water in their favor.

86. Police collusion, no prosecutions, "in the 'line of duty,'"
      vital evidence "lost."

87. "Is a close-up truer than a long shot
      because you see more emotion in a close-up?

Or is a long shot truer
      because it takes in more background?"

88. War does keep the eyes permanently unfocused.
      89. So are we simply prisoners of our world?

90. Mercy fell on death ears.
      91. I lost a sense of what was right.

92. There was a general collapse of civic order.
      93. This chart will calibrate your individual risk.

94. Take the sloppy path between barbed wire fences.
      95. Even a hundred propositions on everyday life

are only a beginning.
    96. Behind the words, other words are unspoken.

97. It all started in shadows
    and is ending in worse shadows.

98. These sudden sprints of loss generally
    outrun the pleasurable wobble. 99. Though sometimes
    the reverse.

100. Anyway, right now, if you're totally
    losing it, you're probably really getting it.

JUNE–JULY 2006; JANUARY–FEBRUARY 2007

# Draft 80: Envoi

So "Yesterday I"
    had a diaristic impulse
        but it didn't work out now.
Or did it?
    July 26, 2006. "Mezzo" what?
Mezzo Nothing.
    Blocked emanation
        of accumulated restlessness.

    Limen, limen.
        Woke every hour on the hour.
Then walked thru the daily
    again, into
        that little littered zone.
And then again; fill in any date and time.
    The flexing of sensation and that oddness
        called unprotected fatedness.
My intangible number of random things
        is ineluctable and yet totally finite.

Interpolates a 3.1415926 on and on,
    scroll of numbers like water flowing
that carry forward without evaporation,
    or, apparently, repetition.

So the universe is based upon a shim,
a particular wobble of atoms
squeezed this way and wiggled that,
almost perfect, almost fitting,
yet absolutely unsymmetrical, inexact.
    In short, it was a day.

And another day, another
        accumulation of those
"striking combinations
        of organic and inorganic elements,
contaminating conventional
        artistic structures
with rebellious uses
        of unconventional objects."
Or the opposite.
        An installation of ordinary objects—
coffee mug, cutting board, bread knife.
        Just stuff lined up upon the strip of life.

Every part of this is inflected by war.
        One airplane flying far too low
                from which I saw and turned away,
a moody child was/ was not unknown,
        gigantic gun that man held up; he'd
                brought a "skeet rifle" awkwardly
into all this; was that preparedness?
        did skeet rifles have so many wires involved, like
                small game traps? it was hurry, harry, hide
instantly, with
        atmospheric stagy unspoken impinging.
                What was happening,
and Who can act? and
        Where is this? and
                Do these parts of speech
mix and mire like piled-up bodies?

There was/ was there?
        gridlock; there was/ was there?
a wound. A fleshy inner lobe be

dripping from, for, over, of and
onto front compaction in my head, and it
reddened what's to see:
prepositional debris.

Most people shadows there.
Trying to seem normal, they begin shaking
blankets in the air and neatening up
those cloudy rooms.
Overcast stitches on the blanket binding
were the work of the dead.
We lie here under them.

                    Wake-up call—
looking for the light, the moment of turning.
Every dawn seems reasonably
        all right, the waft of mist
                the little glitter rearticulating time
indistinct keen thin pinkness
        and participles imbedded, before the rest
                of the day suddenly
becomes brittle.

Dazed. From sheer shadow. And angry?
That this
is not enough? Not enough.
That the force that compels
any investigation
also drives tampering, acceleration,
oil saturating the feathers
of sickened gulls
and the in-
terned.

Preventable pain.
Habitual. Boring to others.
And mainly invisible.

Just itself. The if-self. The
in-that. Pattern—
pattern?
A misty dissolve of mark in all directions.
And if not a flash, a wet suffusion
inside the apparent fact
of surface.
The prepositions gone awry
we cross the site and get swallowed up
by what we inhabit, what we have inherited.

Cloud cascades intensified.
Darkness lowered.
Wind shifts, wind chill, wind shear.
Thunder was starting.
One rumble west, one rumble east,
unusual pressure changes blow and tumble
down the pitch of hillsides to a single restless valley.

AUGUST 2006, JANUARY–JUNE 2007, JUNE 2008

# Draft 81: Gap

Day of Silence, with newspapers.
Pitch. Of silence.

Can one understand it?
    No one knows why.
Aren't there many reasons?
    Yes, but finally.

Can one turn it inside out?
    It is probably irreducible.
    It is impossible in large, and unbelievable in little.

Couldn't those terms also be reversed—
    unbelievable in large and impossible in little?
    But that's not changing any impact.

We had packed the night before because we were due to leave
    so early.
It was cold where we were going, and we were a little
    unprepared.

That saying the name is dangerous and forbidden.
That saying the name is allowed, encouraged. Blessed be the
    name.

These models will help understanding.
These models are derisory.

As I fell asleep, I bit myself.
Therefore I woke up.

But then I dreamed of missing him and her
At the train. So must have been asleep.

We had been planning this journey for a long time or rather
It had come to us and demanded that we take it.

The what is-ness of it.
The nothing is-ness of it.

To understand something, to understand little,
To understand nothing
Can have parallel outcomes.

I asked my friend for some names of people where we were
    going
But she never responded.
There are opposites but no choices.

I thought I could not eat,
But I did have some honey.
We rose much too early.

We made small comments about the road while traveling.
For one, it did not seem in very good repair.

Black smoke poured out of the truck exhaust pipe.
"I'm surprised they allow that."

On the abandoned concrete hut, the graffito RATS
Writ in a brutalist style, last leg of the trip.

What is seen cannot be registered fully
Though it can be placed.

Or perhaps it can be placed
But it cannot be registered fully.

The poisons level off; time erodes something
But not very much.

It seemed normal in an abnormal way.
But that's only because it really happened.

Maybe "normalized" or "normative" is what I mean.
Meaning loses meaning,
But must still be kept in mind.

No one could invent this.
But someone had to, and others entered their premise.
The door was open, triumphant, trenchant,

With acts, specifications, and deeds,
With tortuous articulations of
intricate and particular events.

Stripped stuff in categories,
        And a serious attempt to blow up the evidence.

It is a wall in consciousness of dead air and concrete
        That reads out as fenced acreage.

A box of black for everything.
        What is everything; what is nothing?

The word is a strange word, but now it is bound to you.
Let the word be bound to you, thongs bind the word
Right between your eyes.

This language uses many letters that are underused
In the Anglophone context.
Z and J and W and K. Plus Y. And C.

Wyz could begin a word;
Zczy could be in the middle.

Therefore it looks strange.
One must be careful of certain feelings.

And we didn't pack carefully enough.
It changed to threatening. Very unstable.

What do you find the most unbearable?
This is unanswerable.

People take pictures with digital cameras
So little flashes of light pop out of the dimness.
All the rest were unnumbered, uncounted, innumerable.

Zakaz Wchadzenia Na Ruiny.
Keep Off the Ruins.

People stood in small groups
In wonder. Everything was blank.
But slightly inhabited.

    Ø Ø Ø

Back in town, at the cemetery,
So many pebbles had been put on headstones
That it looked like the graves were piled with rubble.


JUNE 2006–JUNE 2007

# Draft 82: Hinge

### 1.

The book is a mine
of intersections. Margins.
Its inner edges pun on hinge.
The book subsists
by spurt and overlap,
link and lack,
subject and answer,
declaration and perversity.

Hinges are cunning, pegs allowing circulation through notches. A book
hinges; it holds the doors in place so they may open. Like the page, a
cool mist slides down the mountain.

~

The book is a mine
of intersections. Statements.
Thickness implies the combustible.
Sparks catch flame and burn out words.
The fire of the book can even scorch itself.

"We stand bewildered before our own destiny . . . " Perhaps there
should be no more poems, only acts of writing. There would be no
more books, but transfer points; no finished pages, simply work sites.
There would be no more honors because these mainly police, with all
the force of convention, any useful blunder art might make. There
would be questions, and thereupon other questions. There would be no
illusion of instrumental uses and no rhetorics dibbling in frill or decor.
There would be no worship. O, it would be austere and demanding; o, it
would be infinitely interpretable!

2.

Here's a single tangled page that stakes a claim.
Its interplays of hole and hold, of dead and dread
Seem dialectical, yet operate in a structure
Whose tip-top, top-you term I can't supply.

I don't know what to do, how to articulate it.
My stepping stippled feet feel cold.
There are clots in my ear from ashen coals
                            and eyes set deep
                            as refugees
                            in exile from illusions of another world
                            as from illusions of transcendence.
                            Let the head smolder in its grief.

                            But they were only illusions!


～

Here's another tangled page that stakes a claim:
The interplay between hole and hold, dead and dread
Doesn't even begin to represent the tangle—the exposition
Being so complex.
Are you that surprised?

I've jumped on a strange train without checking the schedule for return.
For anything. Outside, darkness, and no one is calling out stations. The
present is dismembered. Undecipherable. The future is paralyzing.
Where are we? The covenant? I understand that it is broken. Look—we
have just passed the scattered tabernacle!

3.

Rubble is continually before me.
Silence of the stalled train.

It lies in its own shadow; the day circulates.
Is this the destination?
Deep in the gutter, my margin split.
The little needle
The patch of gluey parchment
The intelligence of textual scholarship
Can neither mend nor bridge it.
The page falls away.

～

Rubble is continually before me.
Silence. The stalled train
blocks the grimy tunnel,
its catenary off the current.

Wet, my life, and spent in wonder—
was it important? Did it matter?
Who broke these hinges? Who profits
from such resistance to turning. Why block
sorties from side to side, for understanding.
"What's it to you?" Stories, I mean,
There are things for which I am very stony and sorry.

Is there something I need to do that I am not doing?

4.

First, arrive at the spur-line train stop
long out of service, virtually nameless.
A blur of faded letters taxes vision:
sgraffito — scratchy opposite of the readable.

I've heard about ghost tracks
underneath train stations,
where ghost people stand
awaiting embarkation.

-ston  -ville  -tola
-ash. Half Word gaps
get released from storehouses
of half-effaced maps.

      ~

First, arrive at the spur-line train stop
long out of service,
yet expect someone, expect to be met, to get picked up.

        Came tacit greetings from soldiers, but
        I was totally unprepared to encounter this
        "metaphor," and therefore stumbled,
        vertiginous,
        tripping over switches and formidable
        overgrown tracks.

        Day and night, night and day
        *ostinato* continues stubbornness
        in another language.

My heart was in a basket.
Or maybe in a passport.
I fantasized
about carrying it carefully into the woods.


5.

Look, I have carvings here on my hands.
The flesh lines of my palm can be read as letters.

In our writing **H**
on my right hand—
Acca acca acca
Aitch and aitch—
two uprights plus a line of force
zygomatic,
a simple yoke
of satisfying aspirate—
air being expelled in a heave,
loud as a sigh but more ironic.

On my left hand π
something endless that disappears straight into the universe
infinitely, with comic (albeit numerical) glee.

"Eclipse" is related to the Greek word
for abandonment,
although we are not quite orphans
but dots of consciousness
pierced by points of pulsing light
as far away as that
but close as this.

~

Look, I have carvings here on my hands
that open as if opening a book.
    Considering the textures of need and the paralysis of motives,
    considering what could happen in modest fairness,
    the newspaper suddenly stops. But it did not whirl
    as in the movies; it pulled itself together with a sucking in of breath
    and caught itself stolidly against a barrier
    and would not blow away no matter what the wind's direction,
    no matter how battered, partial and twisted.
    That pole was like the peg of a hinge.
    That paper like a book, unbound and bound together.
    It was closed, but it could, like the palm and psalm of the written
    be opened, be regarded.

The first sentence teaches you to read; the second sentence tracks the
surface. Third and you're gone; then you arrive nowhere, in order to
explore what that "nothing" will generate. Suppose you cannot turn back?
Suppose there is no return? Then it is the poem, claiming nonetheless the
interlock and open hope of hinge. For it will sometimes say that there is a
pivot. Yet sometimes there is not.

MARCH–APRIL 2007

# Draft 83: Listings

Really, I could tell you all about me.
    I am 8 eccentrics gazing at the moon,
        the additive surreal and orientalizing.
This girl, that girl
    and her many misadventures.
        Maybe painted
from "memory." Or flung into fragments.
        Is this my book? Wow.

So I became imprudent,
    or even more so.
        Map-like pages sloped downward.
I buried cognates
    in pitch-black narratives.
Have I mentioned
    purling atoms of unevenness?
        the swerve?

I'm actually my own opposite.
    Or even my own indifference.
        A dump. A Funnel
channeling certain stuff,
    unintelligible at some times,
        untellable at others.

Spelling the letters to make words, they really
    made knots.
        These knots are propelled and snarled
by will itself, and by the cunning
    of syntax—
        a force that meddles
with the relations of things.

So I will list my terms:
      pinhole, intersection, hunger.
            Rubble page uncanny.

And the poem will list its.
      Margins. Vectors.
            A crumbled massy space.

Then we will proceed to negotiation
      since both sides demand
            velocity—I mean veracity—from signs.

Worked with gravity, tension, magnetism, vegetables, water,
granite, sometimes wool

Worked in numbers, numbness, puns and patches,
stones, old plates, and bread

Worked by quire, R's, ought, heartbeat, sex,
interlocutors.

Worked in broth, cut, scat, range,
spit, trill, tongue,
and frayed grosgrain ribbons.

Assembled a few relics: Amethyst amulets, Bakelite
bracelets, C and D, the letters, plus lapis and turquoise,
wooden spools now empty of their thread,
lucky eyes, lucky hands, basil, dried,
and alphabet stencil kits.

Worked with mattresses, neon tubing.
Did Color wheels, wove clay.

Extended into Hyperbolic milk stars, into barley.
Split splints, did curl work with sweet-grass.

Worked with clods and clots, scraps, errors,
particularly the typographic,
but also things irregular and ripped.

Worked in off-cuts from construction, in the plastic lashes
that bind newspapers, in corrugation.
Konk! Worked through the simple earnestness of all this.

Worked in standard domestic carpeting, coffee, coal, cotton,
riverbeds and leather.

Yes; worked in and through these elements—
in fold, in small thin pieces of anything
doubled over,
and piercèd so you may be pierced.

Worked through lead books.

What is 40 years? What is 60?

and the despoiling

and the climbing.

Poured over lead pages.

Of, with and after, and thereupon

intuited situations.

Worked trying to suffer—
I mean, to decipher—
the lead library
in the warehouse of unreadable layers,
where every page
is thicker than a knife.

I was burdened with these tasks,
I was aroused by them.
And that particular mix,
balancing possession
with dispossession,
generates the flash, the wake
in the middle of the night—

in the middle of anything.

FEBRUARY–MAY 2007

# Draft 84: Juncture

The Joy's good recipe for bread
had got so stained with flour and oil

that the page looks edible.
Crisp, brown, and saturated,

even perhaps a little rancid
from being so long in the book.

The X's or junctures of this,
all the kneading, the folding over,

the flour-y occasions for tinkering,
for pushing yeast around

are set against an enormous emptiness
that enraptures with its evanescent

loft of otherness
despite congealing into clouds and haze.

And set into a jumpy—really
indescribable—humanness,

desire, enormity, care, simplicity—
random dots against sublimity.

*The reminds me of every*
*thing.*

Clouds are mountains
mountains, clouds.

Where am I?
Under this very sky.

I am "taking," as always, an
"interest in clouds and haze."

Given the toll, the complicity, the inassimilable
surges of intricacy—it's no wonder that

we put that, there or over there at some distance,
keeping them away, when, in contradistinction

everything specified, and everything else
surges into this spot.

There is no there;
it's all degrees of here.

Although gravity is unequally distributed
beneath the surface of the earth.

Sudden ricochet over the swathe
cuts cross a length of "thuh" and "thee."

This will constitute a particular argument.
It will even continue the same ecstasy.

The thrust of th- is argument.
As for elaboration? Development

of this notion? Examples of this
ridiculous, touching proposition?

The difference between <u>there</u> and <u>here</u>
being so small.

And differences
between <u>this</u> and <u>that</u>,

between <u>these</u> and <u>those</u> existing only
(in Eng.) in a suffixial emphasis.

The th- makes semblance.
So pointing is the root of metaphor?

Yet, too, the <u>over there</u> and <u>right here</u>
diverge shudderingly.

The difference between sludge and land,
between drinkable water and not.

Who can then speak of solely
one location? Who, exactly, lives where?

How do I want, then,
to make you understand?

I won't pretend to "make you" anything.
I want you, as I am

dazed by this juncture,
brought vertiginous to this edge.

These days the terrestrial planets
are very bright in the sky—

Mars in the west, Jupiter upper east
Venus simply dependable, silvery blue.

They move ("around us") stately,
one has time, feels one has time

in that situation. But only briefly.
Then comes the sense of desperation.


   ø


Walked and ran by choice alone
through forest, park, and air,

but when I'd got to the faraway lake
to set in ledger—date and name, and place

from whence all travelers had come,
I did not write.

I did not know which <u>there</u>
there was, which <u>here</u> was here.

The juncture where these places crossed
blew through me like particles of mist.

I pulled away and ran far on
without putting down my name.

It was not enough, was not
the book I wanted,

was not the name I is or was,
was not the <u>what</u> I wanted this to be,

despite the fact that I had run so far
and found an open book, which had, and has allure.

MAY 2007

# Draft 85: Hard Copy

"The poem holds its ground on its own margin . . . The poem is
lonely. It is lonely and en route. Its author stays with it."
— PAUL CELAN, *"Meridian" speech.*

1.

17 May 1986.
Or whenever "now" is.
Enough to look at here
For the rest of a lifetime.

Even the simplest things,
Their provenance —
a shoe, a prosthetic
post-war leg
reminding you of
silent doubles
unfinished, imperfect,
imperfect, shadowy.

Slowly the particulars
get scattered to the wind

and one is left
with what is under the surface
trying to come to light
what has not yet
been found nor
been found
out.

"For histrionic or fanatical stress on the mysterious side of the
mysterious takes us no further; we penetrate the mystery only to

the degree that we recognize it in the everyday world, by virtue
of a dialectical optic that perceives the everyday as
impenetrable, the impenetrable as everyday."


2.

Things are very bright tonight—
the city reflects against the clouds.
Shiny talismanic buildings
push objects back into their
specificity, yet the misty
low weather ceiling makes
what we see paradoxically
"less interpretable."
Though I had saved the headlines.


3.

     Emotions wash up and across
us. But mainly impotence.
Orphaned realism.
Instant knowledge, all news all the time,
that's one slogan,
and immobility. Were there other times like this—
over and beyond the bearable?
The question is callow. But heartfelt.

     It surely seems a bloody time—where
someone is murdered down South 23rd St.,
a rough place, disgrace of,
shame of
drugs, deals, rage, and guns,

and then
(today being the Night of the day
war started again),
the shame of War, the one begun as a "slam dunk,"
cabal of manipulation and
devious complicity.

And with no more Time, the vagueness
from which the now vague dead imaginarily
"watch" this
from the outside.
From the other side.
We no longer encounter them

in good conscience.
As for monuments—
see ambivalence.

What is the point of pure revulsion? I am beginning
to be very simple, to have very simple thoughts, no
complicated language, therefore; nothing
too subtle.


4.

It's a question of "among" or some
shatter of the reflection
"to see them"
and "to know ourselves."
The distortion and elongation,
the stupor.
Which is one way or another

we seem to be assassins.
To refuse this "we" —
in one sense easy, and already done,
in another sense
seems almost impossible,
us held hostage to ourselves.

Lie-adept trappings,
Viscous excuses
Snarled-up alibis
bind us to the damage,
And I was
desolate
at this.


    5.

      You and I had crossed that bridge,
the Brooklyn Bridge,
"my" bridge,
together. Then
I said "I want that danger."
Now I am frightened.

Walking through those streets or these. Watching
the marks: trying to penetrate the enormous
sadness. The armoring. The cost. The woe.
Registers of the squandered.
Weakness. Scale. The scale of it all,
and its claims of totality.
Watchers hunch
under the keystone of that story.

Then there is the sudden burst of joy
that it is. That it is. Not as such, not as this
(and it is hard to see without shame),
but that
"being"
remains fluid, dazzling, in play.
The poem alternates among
these states. Is annunciation of them,
these desires indignant for a name.


    6.

Civitas uncanny,
darkened, stippled, riven
with confusion and contradiction.

The dark being both obscurity and incipience,
it's light that becomes
perfectly unnerving.

The problem is to articulate
any promise of the civic,
without this glint of the apocalyptic.


    7.

Bewildering what happened.
The profligate rip of earth, of persons,
of the sharers—plants & mites & languages—
down to the very bit of fleck along the crack.
Is it "your dead" or "you're dead"?
One in the news, or not,

one in some myth, or not—
who no longer finds
credible the humane part
of human nature.

Yet knows in the gut
that something large was thereby lost:
and wants to find it, choose it again,
affirm it as possible.

Open the door
says a weeper
to a stone room,
do not take the path
of the indifferent.


8.

It is astonishing
how much time has passed—
almost forty years, a round figure—
though as time goes, not particularly long.
Just the working day of a lifetime.
To accept that things did happen
the way they did
seems to accept too much.
Perhaps I haven't grasped the necessity
of an *amor fati* argument.
Though what choice is there?
Some fascists will be buried with their Legion of Honor medals.
Some coups and juntas masquerade with "free and fair" elections.

Perhaps this *amor fati* produces what here is called joy.
But still it is riven
with revulsion.


9.

And in this space a birth of enigma
        to which one owes one's own enigma.
It is just what implacably happened,
        and closer up, grief after grief,
error after error, profit after profit, scarification
        and burning. Sharpened on the altar,
the knife, its whetted majesty, is readied
        for another human sacrifice.
What art to make anyway?
        what art for this recurrence?

"The intensity of seeing"
        would be an improvement
                (citing out of context),
as if the sheer clarity of pointing
        the dialectical oscillate of meditation
                could ever illuminate this time and place.
Yet flawless analysis and a temperate
        framing of the stakes
                cannot assuage an other part, one flailing
Being, dazed
        with this particular mood and air—
                with the cold rags of carnage.
    10.

The watchers are struggling.
They're over their heads, have only subjunctive

qualifications, get stunned
in whirlpools of historical sentence,
battered by broken beams and rogue barrels,
as if after a shipwreck.

They are struggling.
And sorry pieces of matter
(children,
children; just
an example)
explore this site.

       A sense of desperate outrage
             anneals the onlookers
             onto the very page
             on which these words are put

as fetish substitute for the directness
of rubble.

"Shortly after the Tuesday bombing, young boys
with black plastic bags moved among the wreckage,
collecting pieces of flesh
scattered around the site of the blast . . . "

       Then closed in the shadows. The world
       made sick
       when children have to pick
       up
       the pieces.

And it's just boys, teasing, or scheming, or
pretending nonchalance, or competitive.
Perhaps sometimes laughing.
For it must be impossible to
weep or rage the whole time through the terrible.
Here are your trash bags. Go forth and fill them.
But is it impossible not to become inhuman?


11.

So—what is the normal?
Speaking to several people at once. Teasing to
some, earnest, flirting, honest, self-conscious.
Speaking as several people at once,
pastoral, neo-classic, professional, sleepless—
the lot.

Well, it's a warm spot here or there.
One street coming round the little square,
the spaces of home perched
variously, with amiable
neighborliness.
In the city. Waverly, right at the corner of 24th.
These pinholes, these spots of light,
as if keys,
open actual houses.

Or the moon, whose warm gold is
actually a street light on the corner
but looking as if it had just risen,
low in the sky, and living

right down the end of our block.

12.

Any consolation that the only typo was in "the father"?
That must have been "the feather"
fallen to the ground
saturnine and angry
from the calling, cawing bird.

And finally I remembered the little villages,
and my long-ago images of great desire,
beautiful city,
multicolored buildings overlooking water,
many entrances, many windows,

but couldn't remember how to get there
and was crying
right in the dream,
weeping and crying
in that dream.

13.

A postwar lasts far longer than they think.
You, for one, will not be surprised.

Torn hope's interconnected-
ness and fallout has become a large and
unyieldy topic.

Being occupied, we try only
to be preoccupied.
Stuff stuff stuff stuff

This is a pretty pickle.
Perhaps the game will
go to extra innings.

It was a Pitcher's duel, turns out.
The enormous fastballs
hit people in the stands.

"Wild pitch, wild pitch,"
They say. "Accident." No penalty.

Too bad. Too bad again.
A diplomatic letter will be sent.

Truce will be declared when
Enough territory has been taken.
Which hardly compensates
for the impact of,
for the depredations of
rancid power

eating away like acid at the walls of possibility.
There is some distance from this to be negotiated.
But only if you're fairly lucky.


14.

She had asked for photocopies

of essays by Edith Sitwell and a few books on H.D.—
and they reached their destination—in Iraq!

I could afford the postage
I could afford the books
And wrote carefully collegial letters into distances
I could hardly conceive of, though
the university, understudied/female writers,
a doctoral candidate, her thesis topic, then her degree
were familiar territory enough—
all lodged or wedged in another world
thereupon become toxic, dangerous.
And so the correspondence stopped.

Is she still alive?
She was very earnest—her letters, pious.
How speak about any of this.
Her opinions about the newest-coming war
were, on paper, not at all like mine.
To the degree, that is, that it had been possible
to speak openly.


15.

I want polyphony
I want excess
I want no art object
No product, no saleables, no
administrative specs, no oversight
of bureaucracies.
I want the wayward and unpredictable
caused by anything

equally stressed, stubborn or obtuse,
companionably destabilized or destabilizing.
I want to make the gesture comes through me
I want to be touched
I want fullness
I want rapture
the erotics of writing
the pleasures of the daze
the over-reach of structure
and the desire for exactness
all sweet together
exfoliating, rolling, roiling through
this "felt-and-fat-and-dirt-and-muslin-maze."


16.

I won't quote a word,
but that notable double-crossing chess game
reveals trouble in the desert,
trouble in the lineage, trouble in the choices,
trouble in the allegory.

What more to say about the Father of everything
from the inevitable, suspicious, atheist
daughter
watching the claim made around the one—
the beautiful, longed-for, pensive son.

They are all male singletons:
one A, one I and one One
(undercounting various brothers
who do not matter in the tally;

nor enumerating most sisters,
though they certainly existed).

Single, except for the One who sent an
androgyne messenger
who rammed the ram into the thicket,
who filled the curly ewe,
who took her mewling newborn sheep.

Thereupon the regime of human sacrifice
was declared theologically finished.
But not politically and ideologically finished.

Clear enough?


17.

Who registers deep lakes of darkness;
Who receives the streak of light upon water?
Who is aroused by the saturated ripples at dusk?
As if all processes could be palpable:
As if this were the beginning
As if nothing had been written
As if there were no tradition
As if there were no traction.
We know this is impossible
But if this were the beginning
What would one want of words?


18.

Stet atrocity

Stet astonishing events fast come ordinary
Stet particular Presidents

Stet plume of smoke
Stet people burn

With an increase of allusions and referents.


19.

Or another answer.
Of words?
Adequate complexity.

People are transformed by the blood on their hands.
Underneath the skin
Self-justifying minor monsters

Harden
Backed by the monsters to whom
Monuments are built.

What one-dimensional sense of Strategy
What Willingness to squander the fodder
What worship of callous outcomes?

What avid and implacable Calculation
What single Illumination
What mono-Ocular blind-sided Vision?

20.

If we destabilized, if
we assassinated, if we bought off,
if we lied about matters of record,
if we set up, undermined, corrupted,
provoked, if we tampered with
ballots, if we used victuals
to twist the convictions of
the starving—if.
What then? Then what?

Then
what will prevent this happening
to us?

Chickens come Home.
And Us Chickens.
Two old sayings.
High crimes and low cunning,
One must refuse. Easy, so far.

Yet a clutch of events
hatches in the world at large
leaving a rash, a stain, an infection, a pandemic.
The haze of power, lures of cheap stuff
freeze the heart and desiccate ethics.
So here is failure. Here is shame.

And the nice life? The poetic vista?
Coziness and connection?
There is no elsewhere.
Even the poem is not elsewhere.

21.

If one began: it.
It was. It happened. Once upon.
Here. Where nothing
Particular is "happening."
Either here or "nearby."
Each stone turns inside out
To manifest atomic openness
As it shows its coordinates,
Thus. To be so. In is.

That stone has more empathy than power.
It does not seek geopolitical advantage
But is simply here, in this, with us.


22.

Some topographies and folds
Cannot be fathomed by the ascription
Of only three dimensions.
This is intended as consolation.
If I were to say all this, all at the same time
The way it's felt,
The page would go black from overprinting,
An unreadable un-negotiable plenitude.
A self-canceling copia.
And at the same time with webby, resonant strings,
The sound would be everything touched, and pulsing
sexually.

23.

Snow blowing from the north plasters the route signs.
What road to take, given
indiscernible numbers and destinations, forks
into little places on "the" way.
And later, still driving blind
sky curdling
with sleet
before I dropped.

There is at once too much
and too little
for getting the force of it, the rebuff
cup of die, cup of day, freeze and thaw.

Such glitter of ice; how did I get here?
This road is so dangerous.


24.

To resuscitate
The covenants that are
Available
To fabricate them as
Humane and secular

And thereby to address
Wrongs of the world, ruthlessness,
Despoiling and injustices:

Is the agenda in front of us.

25.

Walking up and down in it
walking to and fro in it

the ordinary and normal
is the tragic and joyous
is the compromised and the small;
cramped and compassionate
are suffering
and strangeness.

We live in cosmic coincidence
involutedly psalmic
where
"at the climactic moment
the extraordinary place in the second movement
at the very peak of a monumental
orchestral crescendo, the double basses
are suddenly left alone,
impossibly high,
impossibly exposed,
impossibly mournful,
with only a trembling, pulsating quiver beneath them" —


26.

Feeling that pulsation as if in vigil,
Echoing "the cry of human entanglement,"
We want to contribute to the discussion.
We saw the sullying and the malfeasance.
We tried to speak simply
The name of common sense

But were dismissed
As inadequate, discountable, marginal.
Treated, perhaps, as dead.

Now that the moment continues
Can there be new generation?
Is there a beginning? It is an up-swelling
So far not totally plausible. But palpable.
This is tentative; this is qualified.
But the level of crisis is more than we know.
And the alternative?

### 27.

It's hard for me to talk about poetry. Of its particularity. My
sense, against consumable reason, that it matters. So much is at
stake. So many abandoned worksites. The yes and the no
simultaneous. The struggle to repair, even simply to state what
is, how it is, and why it is so overwhelming, with permanent and
never answered questions.

When I meet the professionals whose job is to evaluate
development, aid, impact on health, functioning
infrastructures, and literacy education, who will study the
uneven global distribution of illness, who want delivery of
services, social accountability, changes of policy, who insist
upon small articulations of new outcomes that modulate from
the despoiling outcomes, who want to identify where an
alteration is possible, who want to assess, by firm input-output
criteria, the work that is done . . .

I fall back on admiration and questions. How to make the
confrontation spoken by poetry offer the force of an
intervention—so that one feels the whole

differently. Beyond one, but inside one.

How to talk about the level of art as grounding and arousing. As
compassion, empathy, resistance. As respect for the unknown,
even the unknowable. As entrance into the intricacy of
languages and structures, into the mesh of musical grammars.
How move beyond the "technology of solutions" by making
analysis itself a verbal saturate. How to produce resonance.

So I began writing into the poems
I put words deep into the poems
As into a tunnel

to speak point black.


    28.

The antics of the waning moon at dawn
touching its juicy crescent to the hill
a sudden flare, a sign, a light
upon the nations—
thereupon immediately
changes. Volta! volta!

One sees the earth turning,
one sees time enacted, pivoting.

29.

So she stole her father's teraphim.
What, in the name of monotheism,
was that about?

Those rare black stones.
Sacred knick-knacks, idols,
symbolic lion grabbed at that got chipped,
cover them with the ass of female claim,
settle in for the duration, and refuse
("being in the way of women")
to rise.

Say you are neither disloyal nor pilferer.
And sit tight on the icons and rocks of meaning
gathered from the paternal household,
the talismanic counterfoils, even
the fewest and smallest
from the fierce storehouses of articulation
and defensiveness.
You will remake these goods in your own blood.

"I didn't take enough."
"So go get more."
Tokens from the broken labyrinth.


30.

The distant water
spins the tiny-moon inside whose
shadow was thinly outlined, whose light flickered
like a fizzling bulb, like a spray-of-mist,

like a simile, like an eclipse.
The moon to come
lies dark inside its narrow needle tide.

Textures of incipience and mystery.
Vibration and call.
The light strikes; we read the shine.
Struck like a clear bell,
Again and Again.
Struck words with
Their patchy shapes in the light
Of time, in reflections
Upon day, in the specific
Wake occurring here tonight,
Dark in the garden, debating stars.


31.

There is a space beyond; it has been
called "utopian space" and
we scrabble toward it, struggling
with a twisted goal that presents itself
oddly, like a knot in which
we're knotted.

Is it inside or outside?
Are we both in and out from it?
Are we both made of it and helping to tighten it,
So clotted, so intransigent, so graceless?
Yes. Were I to cry out
full as a symphony, but in a littler space,

this intensity of conviction, this witnessing,
would emphatically signal
unfinished business.


32.

What is important and what is not
in a real place filled with signs?

Night-shadowy floaters, the cloaked allure
of an insomniac mother
checking quiet beds
in dreamy rooms of night,
care and cura
quick foot snuffling thru the house
like a mouse, thru the room
like a worm,

short music
this called vers
long music, symphonic,
the erotics of connection
the longing of zone.

And later, Day-low-violet color, checked out curiously,
for periwinkle or hepatica is the tiniest question—
not socially useful, nor of general interest
simply the name of one small thing
hands on something coming
lips on something other
the yearning to enter

to be entered
and to leap with
desire—


33.

That dazzling blue teardrop
with its swirl of clouds known from here
yet imagined as if seen from above is
imprinted inside us, like a mystery.
We—inundated with a flood of light.
We—"glad to the brink of fear."


34.

To mothers who cannot
protect their young?
They probably know
impotent despairs,
expressed as resignation
but surfacing in little sleights of hand,
candy, or sugar sprinkled
on packaged bright-white bread
spread thin with marge.

To girls asked to filter the universe
by the poets who evoke their beneficence?
What will protect them
from the enormities
that they might suffer in their skirts and veils
while staged on the buffer zone they
are imagined to constitute?

To the little dolly dressed, undressed
in her tiny clothes. Always the word tiny
or little
calls something forth, calls
the all that's never known
into a small detail,
a much-loved ribbon shirred to fraying;
blue and white yarn, the doll frill
kept in that tin trunk made for tea
then taken as a treasure;
the chip, o broken thing! a person able to wiggle
her ears and wink her eyes—surprise! oink!
a little air wherever we are, a
tiny, sweetish song.


35.

The terrible political moment, after the demo,
Though next to nothing was yet accomplished,
When "everyone went home, and no one came back."


36.

Rain cloud caught in the valley
rain falling fast from all directions,
pulses of light intermittent and vibrant.
Despite everything, the instruction
to pull green from yourself.

37.

"A little breath, a bird
        she sits on the edge of the bathtub,
the silence
        where she breathes in and out"

with "another morning
        looks out of the morning"

both may be thought of as defining

an incipience

in tender scale and proportion.
It was what could then be written.

One nano-second later and
a snarl of light that crashed to the floor binds one
to the terrors of historical time.
That's what awe is, that's what fear.
Demanding an intransigent response
To the knife and to its addictive power.

The necessity here still,
Still here.

Of the world's puff and elegance,
        Of the world's implacable substance,
                Solidity billowing . . .

But trying to act
        on this murky path,

overcast wet air, headlines thrown

keeps on demanding other knowledge:
other—unknown, strengths
for negotiating heavier elements:

> collateral wreckage
> > unintended consequences
> disordered order—


38.

The sofa holds a wrinkled nude
Shivering in her blue mood,
Wrapped in a blanket.

A hospice houses someone crying.
Her skin so thin with dying,
It's swaddle-wrapped so it won't split.


39.

Once again a sense of occurrence,

witnessing

one distressed moth,

mottled fluttering

violent, heaving across

the room,

this little life and heart

one street one sign one sight one

desire.

These feelings

of everything

opening straight out into

nothing.


    40.

Can only write hungry
and luminous as phthalo blue

such astringency and tension.
Color as deep as the dream

as incomprehensible
as writing into such time

the work of this time
of making it bear

the nervy weight
of almost unmaking itself.

Lack of a door labeled "door."
And then the lack was a door.

The poem
being archive of feelings to come—

And of what else we don't know.
It is really "quite curious ... "

FEBRUARY–MAY 2007

# Draft 86: Scarpbook

     All of this is part
of all of it.
All part of the thing,
     as in "the thing I meant was ... "

     The blank was drawn
in full sight,
around the dusky dome of time.

It's the thin song of a departing traveler
     hummed as such,
          "the thing, the thing I meant was ... "
over the macro-miles,
     upon the dapple down-draft
          of this apparently sparky endlessness,
small showers of glisten on the visible fluffs of air.

"The thing I meant was ... "
     the cottony cirque of clouds
     is following, probably,
     the line of the sea. What sea?
          Where is this? Where are we?

Bright bits, silence of the real
     register no telling what.
A sense of loss is pleated, crumpled,
     folded into the song. Little floating glimpses
as the clouds blow in the after-flight,
and nuances of city-specific light
     excite the obvious,
     but filled with strangeness.

Thus: perpetual disequilibrium

in the enormous depths of daily
anything.
In the glitter of water,
in wrinkling motion,
    in the waves in the harbor, wobbling suspended
    while albatrosses flash their devastating wingspans.

In the now that emerged from times ago,
the time of Villa d'Este    Staten Island
of "train journey and journey by water,"
    the moment of causeways
    as in the Rockaways
    a train track on a thin bridge
    low to the quiet water—

Yet no matter how such song is primed,
saturate with talismanic words
"fountains, stairways, ferries,
and polychrome money,"
the rest is impossible to recover.

Looking down upon it, above the famous city
    from San Miniato al Monte
    from Maungawhau,
and twirling an undusted globe under one's fingers,
Firenze, sneeze, Auckland,
the data move in vector format
    via incoherent tunneling.
One chancy jot of scratched substance
one classic ponte,
and where did I put my notebook?

How possibly to "begin a journey" when it's
    simultaneity all the time,
how to "write" when there is
    nothing to say but saturation.
"The thing, the thing I meant was ... "

Who knew
    that everything I saw would have proven
        so luminous?
Who knew it would
    prove oneself vertiginous?
        Pitched over the scarp and far away.

Wading into light from darkness, the eyes
    dare themselves to point.
Endazzled by the thing and by the feeling,
    every wall an undulation of umber,
city to city, light to shadow, shadow to light.

Tacking along the edge
in the course of things,
did I really leave
my notebook on that table,
and just walk away?

    Theory is gray, but life is green.
Or was that the opposite?
"The thing, the thing I meant was ... "
this city is "a fire-bed
of 48 extinct volcanoes."
Rangitoto, the youngest,

surprise!
thrust itself up,
erupting right over there in the harbor.
There is no safety!
There's only a kind cut, there's a cold color,
cadmium? electricity?
or rose's tiny field,
humming the song
of the traveler who arrived
disoriented, but here.

Il Papiro is tucked left aside, facing
the geometric mosaical Duomo,
its sweet notebooky smell tempting a person
never again to write another word
because that paper in its elegant binding
is so lush, so finished, so watermarked, so fine
that no one
should ever touch it with a pen.

But Paper Power or a Tapa Notebook
carried writing into other directions
provoking obverse desires —
to pulse from every pore at once.

This debate is like the arc of sky
behind that X-center constellation
(blue giant, red giant and cross-lined buzz)
going from one side to the other

language being the desire to say
"it," and to articulate
(failingly)

the vibrations of luminosity
that saturate darkness
in this zone of enigma.


To see Orion,
now southbound, another shape come round,
    his misty belly sword-stars rising up, not down!
Here's something
    makes my heart pound
and my ears roar
    worse than Sappho's,
who could always demonstrate
    pure desire's paragrams
caught for the moment
    in an everyday spot.


So from this scarp, you'll have the most wonderful view
    over the wobble and far away,
        you'll see almost to the other end of the world.
Whereupon this student proved,
    from his wheelchair,
        that overview poetry ("earth has not anything
to show more fair") was inadequate.
    It was only the hardness of
        rolling through it, of falling over it
could possibly matter.
    Ghost to mist, spark to fire, spoke to speak
        over the scarp and into the light.

And one thing, one thing
    I meant to say was
here is a pocket, here is a passport.
    Here is a tisket, here is a tasket.
Take this map
      been folded back and forth so much
           that street names fuzz and monuments blur.

Exhume the name. Excavate critique. Disinter mercy
for what was lost and far.
    Now let's talk.
    What city would you finally say we are?

JANUARY 2008, MAY 2008

# Draft 87: Trace Elements

The trace is
a hold/a hole
of evanescence through which
travel small powerful things,
impotently, earnestly, but, and,
whether, what if underlying them.
Traces of what happened
commend your attentiveness to the almost invisible.
Since they cannot command.

For once hosed down,
pavement no longer
shows its bloody brown.

. . . . . . . . . . . . . . . . . . . . . . . . . .

Or perhaps trace is readable signage?
Glyphs in day-glo painted on the street,
wiring and piping underneath.

. . . . . . . . . . . . . . . . . . . . . . . . . .

Or it's perpetual unsettling in the
peppy depths of daily
anything, the blur of pixels,
coincident conjuncture,
the odd thing
to the side, dot-detting
like floaters in the eye.

. . . . . . . . . . . . . . . . . . . . . . . . . .

Or trace exists before all this
and beyond none,
yet buoyed
and endlessly impalpable.
Incipient emptiness of a living void.
The chora before concept, the vague where all is one,
that place alternatives collapse,
some space without between.

. . . . . . . . . . . . . . . . . . . . . . . . .

Or trace indicates almost meaningless
propulsions of smudge and grit
dragging vestige, graffito and spoor.
Gray puff of dust at the corner of the stair,
red thread-end from the needle
dropped onto the floor.

. . . . . . . . . . . . . . . . . . . . . . . .

Or—or.

§

Stuffed animal that got
left by accident,
fallen out of and off,
soaking sodden in the parking lot.

The trace is like that.
Lost bunny anywhere.
Forgotten. And not.

§

The map, creased, softened, and re-folded, yet still legible,
   marks

the Trace, specific trail through an exacting landscape

made by the indigenous.

Around the rocks and darks, shades, evanescent but palpable

haunt and lurk, lurch, grimed with visionary grit. With grid.

"Does the researcher have the knowledge and the skill to
   carry out
the proposed research?"

§

I've seen saturated days
where everything is sign:
beech twigs scattered randomly
buckling asphalt where its roots push up

the flash in memory that helixes and strands,
since "each memory is many memories."

§

I've known parallel days of unreadable
alphabets, unutterable
languages unraveling, in which
materials bubble up (from what?

and how?)— an engram sent by chemistry, a dream-plot
out of sedimented fossil-thought,
a locale or event in which there is as much
forgetting, salvaging, evoking, condensing
losing, rearticulating, interfering and mixing
as any single memory trace,
taken, that is, as
actually remembering something . . .

§

You know you are an item in an interlock of items,

but with ecologies of your ignorance, you don't

see this. The political site, here—

thru which a figure loomed it was
some other/other self
a messenger, vocative
with its sing-song accent, irregular grammar,
difficult stammer.

                        Did this get dreamed or where was it?

§

"Is the problem 'researchable,' that is, can it be investigated
through the collection and analysis of data?"

"Was each piece of data subjected to external review? To
internal criticism?"

No. And Yes. Data as every
part of the poem on
every scale, with every layered
possibility for shim, split, and
juxtaposition, that prismatic
-hedron for the faceted refraction
of choices and debris.
These pensive intersections
are what demands research
are what research demands.

§

the girder        amid, between, among, above,
the rubble        under, on, from, next to, within

§

Two shadows blown.
*("every photograph is an archive"*
A word or sentence into void, with sudden gust
*("from the moment of its inception,"*
it swirls back and up. *("it records the past."* Confronts.
Incredible this life in time. *"(at least, a glimpse of it"* Erodes
monuments to scatter, tree to dust. Although "my life takes
time," it is

a clump of mud, a smear of dirt with memories, it has
professions, boredom, preferences, collections, thoughts to
repress, facts unaccountable, a staining over rawness, a light red
brown as the dirt dissolves, oozes into fibers, it may change its
shape, for even after time the residue persists, marked, un-
marked, and thus the stain is ontological, still there though not

there, the shard deep slung, perhaps unfound, perhaps only
intuited, the stain is political, a question of power, the trace is
like a missing cry

§

"Nothing is ever lost" cannot work.
A banal piety re: recollection.
"Everything is lost" doesn't sum
it up either, although
such a suspicion does lurk.
It seems that physics
resists total loss
yet guarantees, with its force,
neither knowable shapes
nor comfortable substances.
So there we are.
And Event may stark you.
Accident mark you.
Hence you can think what you are thinking
only from thought perpetually half-lost
holding out a salvaged half-gone token.

Behind these words others are unspoken.

§

DOCUMENTARY

I am my own stranger,
foreigner of the self.
Citizenship—privileged and suspect.
Passport, legal. Papers, tracked.

Immediate Image Overwrite—Disabled.
Memory size—Standard
        with Built-In Data Loss.

My intangible number of random things
now gone, yet still persists
that tea tin, a little red trunk,
buckled and locked.

"SWEE-TOUCH-NEE": unquantifiable mystery—
pretend Chinese? The trace as
"compact hyperbolic surface"?
The sort. That sort one does
not know is sort. Like learning
what your own child
        actually remembers
                from when she was small.

What? she does? event that
wasn't even "there"
for you. Something
like that,
inexplicably meaningful,
is the trace of what
        you didn't even know you had
                and cannot even now define.

§

Smudged midge or pencil dot
evoking trace—has even

this resolved too much? into summary sign
articulated in a phrase or line?

Is it a visible residue of the mark made,
formulated, and even if blurry, set right there,

or is trace the mystery of the mark erased,
painted over, hardly seeable, barely noted, repressed.

Could trace hover between the two—
made and unmade, bordering on the palpable—but just not.

When "symbols" and "wholes" fall into disrepute,
one has marks, ticks, shards, dots, smudges, soot.

§

Trace is the enemy of fill
        but sometimes it is fill
trace props intensities
        of emptiness open
and generates
particular flickering recognitions,
        but sometimes not.

Trace is not neutral
        no guarantee of purity
trace not ineffable
        trace always historical

but writing history, after all,
is only plausible wager
with interpretative border

on patchy sources, riven
with fissures, alternatives, gaps.

                    This item packed by #4.
                    Thank you for your order.


§

This and that.

The operable site is wherever you are standing.

Through the pinhole puncturing the page,

a murky diffusion loops through undulate Uncanny.

"A visible mark or sign of the former presence or passage
of some person, thing, or event."

What trace is found depends on your readiness.

To a birder the quick swoop
is readable. To someone
who did not look up in time—
she's hardly a feather better
than before.

§

The little bit

to the side, then, the extra letter, the phoneme shifted

on the margin of edge.

Restatement as resentment.

Were as where.

Historical dead for historical dread.

These are the typos of excess as loss.

And the reverse.

And they say—that memory folds over itself
making residue when you least expect it to;
they say that motivated anxiousness up-juts,
and links déjà already view
to things so fast, so slight and so unseen that
you wonder both at crimps and folds of loss
and at intensities of presence so obliterated.

"So I went back trying to find a trace of what had been there."

§

The day is rancid as the year. The mall is filled with things.
Yet there are traces of information, barely articulated, barely
    received.
It's what we miss, and what we needs must have.
For trace elements, the concentrate is less than 100 parts
per million atoms. With trace nutrients, they're necessary
in precisely articulated
yet minute quantities
for proper growth.

§

Ceteris paribus. I mean, things being equal. But they're not.
Keeping variables steady is a fool's errand. The trace and its
undertones emerge as small largeness, and subtext flips to text.
Things being equal suggests that one establishes those precise
things and holds them hypothetically at par. Language surprises
more than this implies. Reality as well. Little abuts large.
The universe is engorged by point or dot. The between
itself travels between. All things being blurry and
      supersaturated
might be a better place to start. Ready and reading
what one can.
All words are calque,
all discourse sedimentation.
Given: that things are mackled, spotted, stained: given
that words are fat and juiced with jargon;
given usage, whisk and turn
plus the odd effect, the dot that wove a net . . .

Given this— Cannot present argument about trace.
We are in another, non-forensic place.

§

This impression on the page
is doubled owing to the platten's
dragging on the frisket.

Quick, to the side. Look!
There
was the trace.

But you missed it.

§

Given the strangeness of writing, the darkness but grayness of
its traces, the acid paper, its unaccountable pulse, the despair of
it, its ridiculous pretense, its evanescence and nobility, its
statistically probable erasure—what?

Between discovering a mini-solar system ("just like ours") with
tiny planets unthinkably far from here, and finding that the sun
will burn and shred beyond the trace of TRACE—Transition
Region And Coronal Explorer—that is, knowing
that pedestrian acronyms will boil right down to atoms
and leave no Earth,
leaving what we would have called "nothing"
had we seen it, or not even "nothing": it's that all our eons
that were known and lived
will just have been
some ashy smudge that's now incipient . . .

§

Watch out; that was too much.
It's hard enough
writing with traces,
alluding to trace elements,
and bargaining with the strange—
without the fact of ultimate loss
untold, untellable, with no ear to tell,
no bell to toll, no sound to read
within the out-flung pitch of cosmic time
except such unspeakable

force or residue as will unknow itself
inside gigantesque vibrations
that we-the-missing theorized once,
once upon a time.

§

This may have happened more than once
and more than here. ██████████████

§

I need not go so far as that beyond to find
the trace continually before me
within my little littered zone.
Thus "imagery" is pebbles fallen on scree
or crumbs of bread upon a trail
immediately swallowed up by birds
whose pecking was too quick and dark to see.

Since seely creatures ate the bits, and stones
have camouflaged themselves on stone,
the easy track to take has disappeared.
And now it is possible to wander
fallen upon hard times,
trying every direction,
repressing every fear,
choosing every confusion
without a clue to "path."
And blazes once-upon-a-time fresh marked
fade weathered on the bark of trees.

§

One I
stumbled thru this
watered-down abyss
graven with rivulets of marking
whose
chryselephantine desire,
whose
golden intentions were
captured in a tracking shot—
compromised nonetheless because the camera
leaked, the picture bleached
and there were lines
criss-crossing the film. So it made no sense
as it spooled out montage.
The narrative was scratches, flashes,
random X's on rectangles of white.

La poesia povera.

§

Not so much the world in a grain of sand
        but the grain of sand in the world
defines trace,

Not to "'express the unexpressible'"—
        poetic posturing—it's wanting
"'to unexpress the expressible'"
        "inexprimer l'exprimable."

But is this too absolute?
Is this its own sentimentality—
this definitional, paradoxical ineffability?
Is this thought of trace
inadequately historical?
Trace so poignant a concept it almost
erases issues
of motivation, of malfeasance,
of interests, of injustice

§

for everywhere, there were
small almost invisible
urgencies, but how to put them together?
this Littleness in just the right amount . . .
trace elements (wiring and piping
priming and writing),
this monumentality
broken and scattered.

For Everything in some
lights represents trace or could become
a trace of something else,
which implies
not that trace
is outside of structure, but that it is
the shattered bits of former structure.
Perhaps the quiet residue of structure,
perhaps some outcast exiles from stricture.
Anyway, a relationship with structure.
It's "Nothing beside remains. Round the decay
Of that colossal wreck" and so on.

This discussion does not proceed by method
but by the sensuality of flash,
the desire to name elements, to show array fanned out
but not assembled, for many are the ironies
of pretending to "assemble"; thus
to fix, solidify, define.
But many are the ironies
of not.
Trace wanders between.
Trace is between
fixed and not,
solidity and not,
porous and not,
open but evanescent, and both ineffable
and, if solely ineffable—almost useless.

§

Better is that tactic of mending the shattered
with lacquer mixed with gold,
producing precious crackle over the surface,
so one "illuminates the breakage."

§

illuminate the breakage
illuminate the breakage

§

Situate the trace as
response to rigid system. If
all we had was trace, we'd have

at least to acknowledge
the need for provisional system

otherwise nothing
can be seen, read,
interpreted or taken in.

Gather and respect the webs of residue,

accept even the whiny vibration of micro-tones.

Thus need a system that "retains discord," moving
the motley processes into emotions of arousal
that precipitate knowing
through longing and
pleasure through temporary
saturation
in its own
metamorphic solidity.

§

Nothing be_side_ remains, and
nothing
beside _remains:_ a grammatical
shift from verb to noun
might be the point.
Reverberation, and the unfixable between.
The excess of the word refuses to forget.

§

"... long-planned refurbishment of Jefferson Square began
more than a month ago, and fragments of ceramics popped from
the ground as soon as bulldozers began turning the earth.
Neighbors scooped up and saved the mysterious fragments ... "

§

Mementos no one else cares for
a pretty bead in an old box
(something about your mother in this)
that you have made survive for now
by keeping it where you are,
and so the trace can cause happiness, comically,
as when memory sees the cute plastic
toilet of a 50s dollhouse or can remember
flashing up a lost evanescence that never
existed, wires crossed in some
capacity that specified
"soup" (the dream of carrying a bowl
of soup up ladder into a dark room).
"Up" means up from where?
The skull as dump turned upside down.
Stand on that hill and riffle through the mongo.

§

The moon is pinky hot and more intense than that,
lavender-bluish delfts the graying sky.
Golden silver apples, planets
and the joy simply
that something apparently beside the point
("There are no truly green stars")
centers us in wonder. "That's so—

I don't know!"
Or seeing anvil thunderheads
loom above the clouds.
And personal memory does not survive.

§

"My hand goes down on the page.

I etch choices of portage, marks of debris, failures of
    infrastructure."

"I rip these images out of the newspaper."

All local and all oddity must speak accurately

Even things one cannot even note

are to be acknowledged in these

approximations of never saying it exactly

but feeling as if conduit for a vast sound

or pipeline to enormity of fact.

*"Who knows this or that?*
*Hark in the wall to the rat"*

Even those who have no praxis,
even the tedious or obsessive, even
the disorganized, those who cannot say things
in the formula "we" say them in,

who are not, as the phrase goes, "in" the discourse
even those handsome and tall as you,
and even those who have drowned in Lethe

might be avatars of a necessary trace.

§

"Theory is made modest and provisional—is rendered in part
untheoretical—while slivers of the practical, elevated to
sustained attention, take on the character of philosophy. Piled
up with fragments and therefore without goals, teeming with
significations that can never be realizations . . . "

"crushed, neglected, inconspicuous"

these trace elements

function like poetry made
by standing where you are
patiently watching and listening,
patience for the layers
in things & words
in systems & syntaxes
waiting for the twist or quirk to coalesce
and signify and turn and disappear.

§

The Purple Hair-streak
        Quercusia quercus
        whose "underside markings,"
a "silvery-greyish ground-color,"

"mimics
        not the green pigment
of the leaf itself
        but the reflections
        of the shiny leaf-surface"
where it might alight,
"and the white discal line"
        "corresponds
                to the highlighted
reflection
        from a
                leaf-vein . . . "
What should we do with that intricacy?
What's traces might be whole ecologies.
What I cannot pick out might be,
gridded differently, the central evidence.
The very word
trace
with its hint of minority and mischance
might indicate our ignorance.


§


Nothing is minor.
It is a positional misnomer.

§


"All the collected shards and fragments were carefully laid out
on cookie trays for the museum curator's inspection. 'They had
buckets and buckets of porcelain and ceramics,' she said. . . .
The area perhaps was used as a waste dump for imperfect
pieces," for seconds or off lots

the poem.
A waste dump for shards
the thing broken in being made
and the pieces mainly don't match
but collect enough and what . . .

§

"We are concerned then
        with investigation." So get
on with it.
        Does the trace mean
only
        what exists as
"present but insignificant"?
        What about the "absent but real"?
What about the glottal choke
        between barely
said and not?
        What about effaced
text, the darkened page,
        what someone blackened out
from censorship
        or rage.

And when the investigator
        (what were the politics of that appointment?)
has read the clues as they present themselves
scattered
shadowy
blurred
inarticulate
        (missing perhaps another field of traces

blinded or entranced by reigning paradigms)
and announces the solution to the crime (or crimes,
for in the intricacy of the <u>noir</u>,
plots multiply, and many are the intricate findings
inter-involved and kited together),
we must be satisfied.

§

Must we be satisfied?
Chemical smoke falls into the ocean, diffuses, the plankton
absorb it, the fish swallow disturbed plankton, then fish are
caught, we eat those fish. And thus we are caught in our own
smoke. Caught, and opened—to whatever that smoke
encompassed in its rankness and gave off when it burned.

§

Yet the Imaginary Museum of the Sardine
exists. And
the Poetics of the trace
is like that.
The sardine is prolific
and nourishes. Calcium, fish oil, protein.
Therefore one may celebrate it.
It lives, they say, in every ocean upon earth.
The trace allows a sight to shape. A more.
The trace is our ancestor (as the museum says
of the sardine); it retains its secret side.

We will show you the fundamental role
of the sardine/of the trace
in our mental universe

in the Imaginary Museum of the Sardine.

For the Imaginary Museum of the Sardine
does exist. It does, it has
a flyer, a brochure, a little dépliant
from France. From Sete, in fact.

Illumination Intérieure—
mettre le visiteur en situation de sardine.
And the museum has collected
a thousand cans
from all across the globe
exemplifying how sardines are packed.
L'exposition qui fait parler les sardines,
where sardines get to tell their real stories,
so to speak.

§

For traces caused by enormous historical crimes

one thinks, unthinks, and thinks again.

Molecules remain in air. We breathe each other in.

This is not consolation.

The present is dismembered;
we pass into a long tunnel
our ears are stuffed
and for seeing, it's only the sepia reflection
of the same car
looking in on itself

thru the dark in-hill corridor.

To evoke
that particular airlessness, do
I manipulate the tragedies of others?
Is this narcissistic claim?
At what point in the dictionary are their words

mine? what rhetorics
precisely won't suffice?

§

What was it? What did you want?
"how to tolerate an inconsolable instant . . . "

that has spread its wings
the spiral of gravel kicked out underfoot

and the charred book
the meltdown of page in the world's greatest age

the Age of Ash we are
the alloy of.

§

What can be witness
after the eclipse of witness.

In the axial light of early morning
        I pulled
one eyebright from the fascist field

and called it a forget-me-not,
though this was not its name, but
just for being blue.

At the end of that day
all dried and shrunk,
it turned to powder in my pocket
and still is there today

perhaps.

§

The names that cannot rise,

the dead and their graffiti.

Call them Call them

from Tanglewords on the wall. Pick your own detail.

from buried documents suddenly found,

from seepage of poison in the ground,

in the ground and in the flowing water,

and from invisible insomniac twisting.

Trace is evidence.
It is a blurry mark of what we should have known,
and did,
a melancholy reminder

remaining unresolved.

Trace offers flakes of the unimagined

and unimaginable so we can

continue, fully unable to imagine it.

Or unimagine it.

§

The traces of the missing and absent
The traces of present and palpable
misspelling mementos as momentos.
Crossed products with continuous trace.
Presence and absence turn each other
inside out and over, entering into each other.
It is impossible to "finalize" trace.

But trace is a poetics.
That's one thing one could say.

So
to gather up
to speak of traces, don't be sentimental.

Otherwise without this ambivalence
to its evidence,
a reading already saturate in the ethos
of the evanescent mark,
trace will get too plump, or some symbolic
stagy gesture will smother it. Stop romanticizing

trace. The point is that trace
queerness/ nearness/ sheerness/ mereness

is a smaller rhetoric than seems plausible.
It is modest.
It is almost uncontrived. It makes no claims
                            that it will survive.
                            But in its abyssal elation
it offers "a fleeting
but sharp pulsation
of historical awareness."

§

Thus some say poetry
holds the trace in some permanency,
frames the evanescent flicker in,
as if language produced aura in real time
and sensual memory were always active in a work.

But a poem may end as oily blot
a frayed defeat
shredded, burnt, flooded, forgot,
kicked into the trash by heirs,
like ancient papers on the archive shelf
sold, and ripped, and twisted into cones
for holding *frites*.

§

one must respect the traces of others as one's own.

Trace the stranger pulsing
on the hearth of heart
its particular flame is votive.

It is information of our own existence.
Generating and interpreting the scraps
and hearing our little tunes
becoming this,
and there are other sounds
swung hinged
in the woods, too

that come to me and to you
from (Y)-i-o-u
this way.

§

"the fragment is an indispensable thought form . . . where
the break occurs—where the fragment breaks"
in which and from which we make both system and singularity
we make sensation that resists a system

"the intemperate presence of the micro"-substance.

So any dim poem might not be the place,
but poetry offers one plausible [cross out ~~shimmering~~] site
saturate with trace elements.

§

Abandoned among detritus in a plundered world,

we are the traces we seek.
We are our other otherness, and others are (in part) our selves.

The page turned black from burning, from overprinting,

from plethora or spill. To see the trace is to acknowledge this.

Imagine the reader who
would persist and still persists
Something so small; something so large; how to get a handle on it.

Nomadic smallness in the workshop of abyss.

Must fail, must fail as a practice, yet must accept this with the

fullness of being. Then self becomes the trace

and knows the trace thereby.

§

One word, with its history, its specificity, its residue,
the scintillation of its distractions can open a universe
of connectors. That poetry
being words is like this, that poetry is made of trace phonemes
trrrr or eeee or clicks and swivels, and historical
evanescences, and even unvoiced schwas
that speak, do speak with palimpsested distinctness,
but at the same time as opening
we wonder, with the blockage and closures of words,
how anything is understood

between people, her twisted lip and
overcompensated speech, his deaf ear,
an unfamiliar accent,
the static of the room
humming with a ground noise:
"I can't really hear what you're saying"
a panic of the blurred,
of the cupped ear.

That the loss is palpable with each use of letters
or the sound of words
that the act of writing is, hearing is
an endless melancholia that is happy, that is alive, vibrant
joyous with the irregular pulsing of
such findings.
The sadness is alive inside me!
The trace emanates traces!

§

Because everything may have meaning
every mark, dot, swirl and particular color
indicate steps to the hidden water, to the story
of that water, to its ancestral land form maker,
trace is inscribed everywhere
and the world is trace,
but without the reader.

Without the reader, without translation,
without the listener, without decoder—
nothing.
                    And each letter's tangle
                        caught like us, itself at the middle

of one dark word
> after another, its black iridescent sheen
>> activating multiple angles
>>> for interpretation.

Hence reading
"the book within the book"
becomes a manifest.
We are custodians of the meanings
we make of world.
It is circular,
this argument, if it is one,
but to pine
is ridiculous.
This is
trace at its best.

§

Let the shard become readable by
jaggedness and by piecing,
let letter engage its crowns
let black be luminous with luster,
let the mote on the scroll fly up and open
as the scroll is unwound like a bandage on its bejeweled
     rollers
let the naked scar of text reveal
the eye that stares back into eyes of ours.

§

All serifs are seraphim: such is faith in the letter.
Such is the force of the word.

The faith is touching.
In every alphabet
in every technology of memory—
knots, rocks, dots, rhymes,
codes, rites,
monuments and books—
in that shockingly endless tower built
of the balances and loops of wire
ceramic shards set in cement, and mirrors, too,
extendable yet poised in mutual
enjambment—
oh.
There is no verb in this sentence.

The verb is diffuse
it is the feeling of Being
and Reflecting
inside the substance of language
and of time,
making the poem "embodied, embedded,
and extended mind."

§

What else to say? Each mark persists as it can

in its particular existence. Someone works

at reading it, at acknowledging it as different, as difficult.

Sometimes languages, sometimes

reading skills. That smudge on the wall
is in fact folded inside thick intricacies

of rune and turn
of ruin and tune.

§

So the trace is exigent,
even if almost obliterated,
even if we know it only
as something on the verge
of its own disappearance,

the trace is exigent.
It has demanded
at least this.

FEBRUARY–JUNE 2008

# Draft 88: X-Posting

free variation on "Keine Delikatessen"
by INGEBORG BACHMANN

X at that place where there

are long tables and platters of food.

Some throwing selves eagerly

into the banquet of engorgement.

There was patent appetite, was simply

wanting more, as if innocently,

were self-fed patches of avidity,

fashions of hysterical attraction

to largesse. To largeness.

Ate through that buffet, falling

on the array as if we'd never eaten.

Plate after plate—such fancy things,

smoky, salt or sweetened,

crunchy, costly, lavish.

Because this did not nourish

we stuffed and ate the more. Oh yes.

And then the shock.

To have ingested this as such

To have swallowed it down.


*Without delicacies,* without delicacy,

no rhetoric either

and certainly without refinement

I stand before you

foreign and distant,

(although near and constant)

wondering

whether any part of this is worth it.

Questioning

whether I feel anything

I can talk about, and

whether thinking about feeling,

were I to bring myself to "do" it,

to make that effort,

is particularly worth it.

What is the force of my conviction?


I have no appeal in the court

in which I am standing.

I seem to be sentenced by the sentence.

So what's the compulsion makes me

begin this debate yet again,

either to stuff it to *Metaphor*

forever, or to stuff it full

of Metaphor, tinkering around

with such skill in finding likenesses

as once I might have gotten praised for.

Who was that self?

It isn't as if this "I" had gotten nowhere,

is it?


Should I dabble onto easy easels

all the pretty little *pictures*

that used to give such pleasure,

*almond blossom* petals as my brush?

Mandel-baum, Mandel-stam, Mandel-stein, Mandel-brot.

Almonds

are motivated by the names of people I remember.

Once I was malleable as marzipan—or

rather, I let them think so.

But Who are you? I said to me.

What do you do it for?

Should I continue *bending Syntax*

to these uses? What uses? Such scintillation

I could certainly still produce:

with all the skill in my sparkle kit

so you may admire

my hyper-sensitive yet completely

idiomatic performance.

What a showing I used to make!

But what could I do with it?

What should I do about it?

Who is that self that ever wanted to?


Am I the one making the work

that seemed endlessly

to flow, bubbling, babbling

Pavlovianly

whenever someone bonged the bell

called "Poetry."

Who cares about "Poetry"

after hours at the bus stop

when the dragged-out, dogged ones

with their bulky shopping bags and swollen legs

have the bus lowered for them?


Angry

    Resigned

        Disempowered

            Making do amid this *Schande*


Murky near and murky far.

Disruption, Hopelessness, Malfeasance, Fear.

Isn't it plausible to feel

impure, baffled, resistant to "the literary,"

ensnared and burdened, split

into resistance and identification,

with chronic entrapment, panic, the incurable,

with fixed-income poverty, terminated benefits, with all *the*

*Costs of Living revealed* to me?


So should I consider

that the Words I was called to write

help others? Was I going to be a Helper?

This thought seemed as bad as all the others.

Was this some Rhetorical Bureaucracy of

Social Worker tasks?

Hardly.


It was *costing me* an arm and a leg,

*an eye and an ear*, precisely that

eye I suddenly saw with,

that ear they all said I had

my beautiful pitch

(but my ears actually hurt), that

leg, that broken leg (and spent eight weeks

on crutches

and was disabled instead of being "normal"

whatever means "normal" with its mouthful of Words—)

—*should I try* to do some good?


There are plenty more pleasurable paths

for me to take *in writing,*

But these seem to be ploys only,

defensive, decorative, deflecting.

No sentences can be made this way.

Sound founders, kitschy gabble.


So do I have to continue?

I feel shelterless,

I feel that the stakes have changed

and I can't catch up.

And then I could not say one little word.

And felt compelled

*to rip up the page* and turn from these pronouns:

I? you? we? Who cares about them!

Who cares how they are linked!

Push them over a cliff!

Which then would leave me with nothing

and with no one

in this reckless space called

no where.


Nevertheless.

What is the consequence of responsibility?

Where is mine?

My side of it all, this itself,

you could gloss,

has made me overwhelmingly forlorn.

I'm torn on these barbed questions.

Whatever I've said —

*take it all as a Loss.*

JUNE–JULY, OCTOBER–DECEMBER 2007

## Draft 89: Interrogation

*Why did all this so affect you?*
The thirst in every direction.

*Where does one go from here?*
This was not intended as an impasse.

*Are you ready?*
Never have been.

*Do you claim you are the author of these terms?*
No, this was something beyond authorship.

*Were you glad to submit?*
It became a condition of my employment.

*Answering to what, exactly?*
Two words, a poem of hers once: "cold ashes."

*When did this happen?*
This time long ago, but still this time.

*Is this your actual level of despair?*
Sometimes, some places. No. Yes.

*What kind of confession is this?*
I am confessing nothing, just stating some facts.

*Don't be naïve.*
I can confess to that.

*Where did you hear this?*
On the web, in the air, over here, over there.

*You seem to listen preternaturally.*
When I heard her saying it, it was as if I had said it.

*So you have made a true statement?*
I don't know; it's a statement come from somewhere.

*This has too much vagueness: somewhere, sometimes.*
I am just answering, you are asking.

*Yet this can't summarize your real opinion.*
I don't want to give up poetry—

*And she did not give up writing . . .*
but every day I give up on poetry.

*Why do you say this? It seems sentimental.*
The adequacy of language produced, and language received.

*Is it possible to know what might be found here?*
Someone twisted in self-interrogation.

*What is the method?*
Why here, why this, why now, why me, and what is this?

*But you say this isn't written in your "voice"?*
No. It is not, and it is also not not.

*So you are lying.*
In this case these terms cannot remain absolute.

*Don't you repeatedly invoke the term sincerity?*
I have been suffused with something authentic.

*But this is not yours.*
It is now.

*That is a shocking statement.*
Though I was not ever like that, the early style.

*What do you mean?*
I was neither metaphoric, nor fluent, nor rewarded.

*Then why make this claim, why use it?*
It comes from a place in me that is a place in us.

*When you ventriloquize her, doesn't this raise an ethical question?*
Yes, in that the thinking comes from between us, an ethical
    zone.

*Who is us; how can you use this word repeatedly?*
You asked the question, that at least was right.

*Would she accept this poem, given what you have added?*
I offer apologies, respect, intransigence.

*Then you are speaking only to the dead.*
I am speaking only to or from the Call.

*"Death is the mother" of poetry, or "of beauty,"*
*whichever comes first?*

No, everything is the "mother" of poetry (like vinegar?),
the merest flicker to the side is, don't you see it?

*Do you think of yourself as her equal?*
I think of myself as your equal.

*You are putting yourself on the same plane with her.*
This is an accusation? We both lived in the 20th century.

*You have appropriated her poem, even abused it.*
Between the points that shift

when I listens and you speaks
we both wander a third grammar, a *tertium quid.*

*What did you seek to accomplish by doing this?*
To touch the wires between us along microtones of pitch.

*What do you mean by "between"?*
This is the hardest to explain.

There is a sense beyond empathy
where some pain and rage simply enter you.

*Are you saying you don't feel empathy?*
I have empathy. I am talking about a visceral sense

beyond, where the universe and the political facts
and the particulars of shock and numbness cross and meet in
     you

making an entanglement or a net of entrapment
that the word "between" begins to answer for.

*Do you enact this "between" in your actual life as lived?*
Sometimes.

*Only sometimes?*
Sometimes only.

*Doesn't this indict your stated goal?*
At close range.

*Why not draw on other theories of poetry*
*—pleasure, elegance, wit, affirmation?*

Take nothing for granted. We gather up our
nothingness and wait inside the unbearable.

*So is this "depression"?*
You have learned nothing.

*You mean to back away?*
No, really to begin.

*How can you possibly continue?*
We all have unfinished business together.

*Doesn't your cogito depend on the silence of others?*
No comment.

*What do you suggest?*
"The whole/ language to/ unlearn"—have we unlearned it enough?

*Are there any auspicious signs?*
This work; is it delusional?

*You are answering questions with questions.*
There's something wrong with that?

*Is this an interim, or is this the real thing?*
"I still haven't been able to figure out what happened here."

JULY AND OCTOBER 2007

# Draft XC: Excess

"What is this that wants this?"

I.

The portal has an electric eye.
Glass doors slide widely
to aisles piled high.
So much to buy
pitched right to you
from these well-stocked Stores.

The filiated You of
threads and links gets snapped.
Embellishments
of greed and feed
blandished by
metastasizing Screed
colonize your micro-bits
by blips inciting urge.

Product flags boot up;
claims stake themselves
across pocked surface "You."
You have no unchecked space.
Speak? To whom? Of what?
Open your mouth,
they'll have you
in their database.

Words? why even
say them, as they fall aslant
of it, of glut,
buffeted and baffled

by things without provenance,
all sleek and shiny bright,
their Shadows
photo-shopped out.


II.

These Words and any words are waste. Are loss.
Improbable Babel left in rubble.
This poem almost became its own erasure.
Almost blanked itself out.
But it's to see those shadows
that this is.

Let in fissure, fracture, broken shard, let the dark costs
                    in.
        Compound the feeling. Deepen it. You have reached me,
        overwhelmingness!

My excess gathers shadows in.
The dark thought bleeds over the four margins
of the page.

Talk to the self?
Small, with sweetish scenes,
its language isn't equal
to its soc-pol fullness.

            Here is a basket full of keys. Of keys, but will they
match with locks? A suitcase without wheels—throw out? or
keep? You can see right away the simultaneous overloaded

presences, the multiple dissolves of "me" in situations. And
that's only the beginning.

Talk to others—
the scattered remnant of
zeugmatic
companions?
            A file cabinet—papers! unsortable! their very there
with spatter lines and cryptograms, you get the general idea of
idems in a series shot through with inexplicable recurrences. A
splintered apparatus. Get a grip!

Talk to the dead?
One friend got up
to tugging at that door
but there was medicine and luck.

            Moon-ruffled, the cloudy balloon rises over the
horizon of cloudy dark. It is all untitled and constructed of
fragments. And of dicht, the density. Moon emoves. L'ight or
Lighn't. It was always like that. And
that was hard enough.


    III.

Talk to the interstice!
To those inside the cost.
That is, to us. Ourselves.
Talk to the loss.

It is impossible to resist
speaking of being here,
whether we have come
too late or too soon.

On the unsealed pine lumber
a dribble of resin
oozes from the darker pores
of knot that had been branch.

Excess: Hermetic clarity.
Excess: Lucid intricacy.
Excess: Multiple interlock.
Take Excess back.

Excess is the lexicon.
The fullness of the word
refuses to forget.

How speak where
rare earth riddles
have no end?
A turn, a fold,
a pitch, a bend.

Excess: the Verb
without a verb,
the Noun of all
and none,
a no and yes,
a rapture
and a doom,

available
for draft
by touch or call:
never, once more,
again, and all.

JUNE–NOVEMBER 2008

# Draft 91: Proverbs

To pass a successful night in the forest, don't sleep in the clothes you cooked in.

We are living in the incalculable. Passport may not work.

A lump in the throat is never food.

Sometimes there's a loss of a sense of the verb.

How even is with odd.

A book: transparent pages, opaque letters, and errata.

Worship is a sinking ship.

Always calculate the cost of whiteness.

When flooded with shame, endure.

The ones who broke the hinges should pay double fines.

Zim-zum, strum, strum, zero sum, wikipedia.

How many times can books talk about books? How many stars are in the starry sky?

The torn are always laden with further burdens.

Birds of a schnozzle flock to the nozzle.

Shake it upside down; you will see capital falling from the Capitol.

Make the book an imitation mountain, but with real hard
strata. Data.

Work is struggle in time with plenitude's scarcity.

Departing can be arriving.

This entanglement reveals ever more attractive labyrinths.

The beyond is in two places: here and there.

Whenever there is critique, there is a third grammar.

To read well, you must open the whole stained cloth.

When dreams are as real as the everyday, one is reading a
higher order of clues.

The Spider poisons for only an hour; the Justice Department
saturates.

Clean the lanterns once each year.

We need a last person singular.

To write is to choose.

Think of yourself before you obey.

What is redeemed is but a token of a token.

Though always on time, you must run for the train in your dreams.

One can never stabilize the line of signs.

Better to have agon and discovery than the guidance of beneficent spirits.

Better still to have gloss.

When π is solved for, perhaps there will also be justice.

If legible, find the illegible in it.

The Global Leader in Portable Blank Media could be You.

When people burn schools, cry out.

Let the mite live. Let the girl become literate.

Economic bulimia equals social anorexia. But who is gathering up the vomit?

Even picking every 7th word is not random.

Take this question as your conceptual muddle.

Bends should be tied only in two ropes of the same size, stiffness, and smoothness.

On the other hand, not everything is rope.

Deep back in the cobble of languages, knot and knife are linked.

Thinking is a problem in knowledge.

Never believe the word "disinterested."

Not hero, not polis, not story, but it.

If you are on crutches, people will talk louder to you, and more slowly.

Wild horses wouldn't melt in my mouth.

Language wants language.

Write only hungry sentences.

Do not always finish the same book.

Look down. Look down, your teeming site.

Can complexity be fathomed without personification?

Even the air you cannot breathe remains your only air.

To redeem the pledge, offer thirsty animals water.

When the government can read your laptop, it's time for cryptography and resistance.

If Duchamp is turned on his head, he is a unicycle.

"I give to you a paper of pins." This is it.

There are red and yellow and blue. Then there is the
unidentifiable "sad."

Don't bottle honey in long-necked jars unless you own a very
long spoon.

If rhyme is the motor, what is the machine?

"The implication of this gesture was enormous": never again
to use the word "gesture."

Look into your own heal and ride.

Reduplicate the awkwardness.

If given text in a dream, try extra hard to read it.

If you are a match, will you donate?

One one-off at a time keeps people in line.

Spotted dick is an example of a cultural difference.

Make sure the main socket has an earth-wire.

If you dream of numbers, watch out.

Keep things cut back or your hill will become bramble-thorns.

Things suddenly happen on a bed.

Integrity in the micro-space is seen from the stars. But even if it isn't!

Winnow the old words; harrow the new; seed from the few.

Adding sugar to make wine is not illegal, but think twice.

Pitch knaves.

Deep back in the cobble of languages, knead and knock are kin.

Plant trees, but also water them.

Gamble only on Language, that wager well beyond Pascal's.

When Serifs get deployed as Law, back away slowly, but always face forward.

Stand forth, mystery. Learn mobility. Learn humility.

Even if you sing a little, little song, still are the words behind the song you sing.

Much obliged. Obbligato. Obrigado. Say it.

Dog's letter for the wonder of it.

No matter what, it cannot be called back.

Is it possible to say what else might be found here?

Don't listen much to other people's rules.

Hold out the cup of dust; show it to those who control water.

Resignation is anger spread over long, lonely acres.

Wake again into the wake of watchfulness.

AUGUST–SEPTEMBER 2008

# Draft 92: Translocation

"Well, they are gone." Nyahh.
"And here must I remain." Yeahhrr.

So, were they totally right, those friends
Who said "poem" — any thing of that sort, was only

Elegy? And to accept it? Was he, for instance,
Really right, who talked of the center

And how I wanted it? Is this, anyway,
Related? Elegy and center?

What is it to claim title from
Unsolaced sets of human webbings?

What is it to be responsible
Dinward to the situation now of which

Is hereby spoke, perfect clarity—joke—
Made up from our so-called national tongue.

And from its foreignness. In dis-ray location.
Where am I? Here. But I don't know

It well. What is it to go beyond recto
Though not by turn or flip to verso page

But to a sonic page called vertigo, of
Nasal quaver tilde, glottal swallowed schwa,

Even the rolled, tongued rrrr which I
Could never do but someday hopen to.

See this? Hear or not? Was this a dream or what?
Is arrangement the dream of a center? Is

It derangement? I wanted
No center. Beyond center was

What I want and wanted. Beyond
Consolation. "Unlikely smatterings of themes"

Emerged from the warehouse of suspicion.
All they went, but must remain here I.

Meanwhile friends, whom I meet never more once still
Upon flexible heath, can, along the edge of summit

Present. And Now, whenever that might be in these
Untoward, nervous, tense-mixed tides and zones,

My friends continue walking under the sky dip
Still on broadly blightened view de-steepled meed

Yet without centralizing Verb's or Vista's
Clearest claims, but simply passing spaces

Through along, in there or thereabouts, through time.
Or seeing her old house, moved off to here by truck.

We found it where it translocated to,
Visible, beloved, and then depart again,

A walk, a ride you'll never have been sure to take
Or taken, slaked, with comes and leaves and finds.

Which way did they, long time ago a-way?
Who picked whatever path to take, whichever

Way, all stranged? With invisible disappearing,
The last seed crow knocked its straight lines awry

Used dark air to-toward far away from yon
And flew beyond. Seed crow? Now is another.

We passed plastic flowers
On the grave of "Buster."

This history, the real true story of intricacy
Began-begins when you-thou thought it done

In foreign selves who live aside the known.
Withal no noise is dissonant.

It told of life. That is, Announced.
And therefore trek and trace the other side.

My period eye is filled with blood.
Like veins thickening, like railroad tracks,

Transmogrified Machines of warehouse
Round us—ducts and pipes. Its knotty floor was

Varnished before sweeping, so that every bit
Of dust and slice and scrape and dirt and dreck

Spreads under glassy surface to stare up
At life in All this Vast expanse of Loft.

And shining! Shining with imperfection!
Silvery clots in open spots of knotholes.

So whether the past or the future arrives
First in sequence might half-sometimes

Be debate. The last ditch, the stand in the door,
The thing declared over, finished,

Was beginning something else another.
Constellations of entanglement, loops and ties

We didn't far away attend
But now and here we recognize.

AUGUST–NOVEMBER 2008

# Draft 93: Romantic Fragment Poem

Follow, fellow, and furrow
this labyrinth scratched in mud,
the "I" I am, the "I" I was,
the I that she collects;
the you and youse
for mulching roots:
yes, follow, pronoun, find and
grasp the all that lay outflung,
the we that formerly
got trashed, half policy, half chance,
our numbers up, like die;
and others, such as they and he
who has and is and are and give
a ritual possession of some spot
that's not a firm R-ticulate,
nor neither fixèd find, but wobbled
floppy thing with ties nearby
—the road, the dirt, the park,
the lot, a thing a-traveling, a pocky
prickly skin of bllod ty3pe O,
some certain bones
and one reverberant
titanium rod, whose
tuning forked to pitch of A
got embodied
and embedded
in the homeless
wandering
poem

as everything. In history.
Sidereal. Unsure.
It could repeat, and had resist,

could then recur, this mangy mongrel itch
for different shapes, for
further speckles in this
rash of textured specks.
O glamour of interior skylines, to
grasp and face this space between,
the space within, the deep aside beyond
whose yearning
activates a crucial urge
along the diva diptych of the page—


those floating motes of light or dust
caught for instant instances before
they changed, yet tried to
fix one there as you,
a you absorbed, an other I,
all this as if some kind living
hand burst up through pressings
of the tissue paper page,
mesmerizingly engaged, wanting
to warm you eye to eye, meet hold to hold,
thrust sweet to sweet, take verge to verge
throughout the full and endless here—
where then abruptly thereupon . . .


MAY–DECEMBER 2008

# Draft 94: Mail Art

Mail Art is/was an international artwork activity, emerging from movements like Dada and Fluxus. It was a communication and gift exchange, before internet and email, sent through the post, in which every aspect of the communiqué (from the envelope on in) had a collage aesthetic and playful, verbally inventive, and jaunty elements. Among the features that I can't replicate in this work are the joking extra postage stamps often from odd countries like Canadada, the rubber stamps all over envelopes, the extra-national postal services (Fluxpost), and the textual materiality of the collage. This work is an homage to and recollection of Mail Art from inside Drafts. In this book, the publishers and I were limited to black and white presentation. Hence this is a selected Mail Art.

# the *literally* mail:

anything—envelopes
scribbles
sealing
labels
certification
cancellation
delivery

correct postage ?

according to the weight of insouciance

*tangled
in the long vigil
of the page*

random lines
burning and dodging techniques
non-silver printing

a monument to any day
half-hazardly

OFFICIAL PHOTO  No DUPLESCIS

Traveling crawling reveling revealing

«ICH»

The predominance of lines was an international phenomenon

*and words: Their Iqden socio —Twisty selves*

listening differently
I got off the train and… This double function can be found in
as the meandering seam of the femak
beginning again what

Sonorlette bedeu.
lockeren Zusmmen,all-encompassing development. Whereas

de cette dimension, il n'y a rien d'autre
à faire que de "composer", qu'on se trouve impliqué dans
multiples that cannot
attach the points there are
however many hypotenuses
one postulates, that go cross every X
and every T, that triangulate
even things one cannot even note.

*simultaneously lead an independent existence.*

Mein Interesse gilt der Suche nach deren Sonorität. Die Idee mit

BAGGAGE IDENTIFICATION TAG
For this reason, they avoid a layered pictorial structure with

women leaning out of the cabin window as well

VIA

VIA
replaced underperforming managers,
and redefined the company, aiming it

VIA
0220 702246
but it changes for every event), there are others,

# en dialogue avec.

[149]

**SHIVERING AS HEAVY RAINS COME DOWN,**

**ALPHABETS BLOWN AT MY HEAD, PRIOR TO DEFINITION**

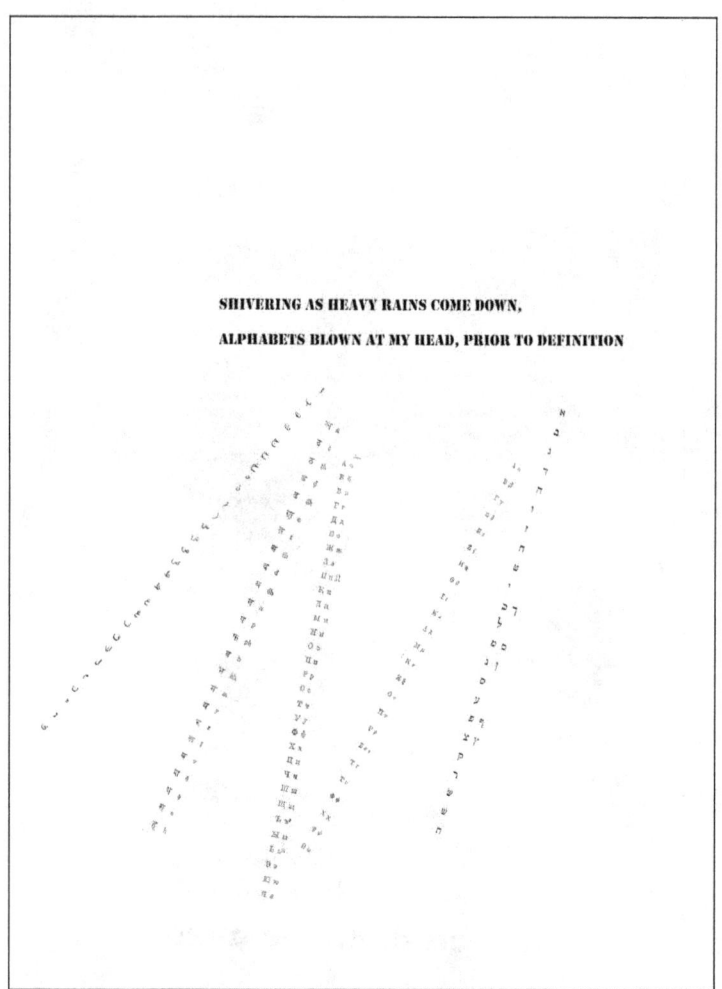

```
turn AWAY from
turn AWAY from
        the buying
        the using, the destroying
        the unfulfilling

the insensate
the lack of empathy
the instrumentalizing
the damaged sensibility
"these drastic fucking times"

no grandstanding
regain!
regain!
The sun hums with a million tones, solar max in meets and bounds.
```

A single letter, black flake, blows back against the page.

*Shabbat tractate, 115a*

*Shabbat tractate, 115b*

talismanic
Talmudic

R   EST   LESS I was late for the appointment,                was trying to map a drive to
where, where was the place I was                     going? sets out the typos of excess
breakable code dismembered words What is, is. What's
       torn is laden with further burdens,
                            even if there are again 7 new days.
                            Thus one enters one's own life as a traveler.

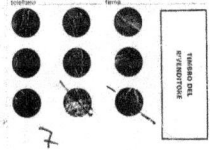

7 new days

Even a nothing, the ur-dot
Stood
not majesty, not overview
but dot to dot, and mite to mite
 "every discomfort produces desire"
inundated in a flood of light.

Make a shape for the day.
I want the diagonal.


YYY
 If there were holes cut in this page
(not impossible)
what would be the word groups
underneath?

underneath gets better and better

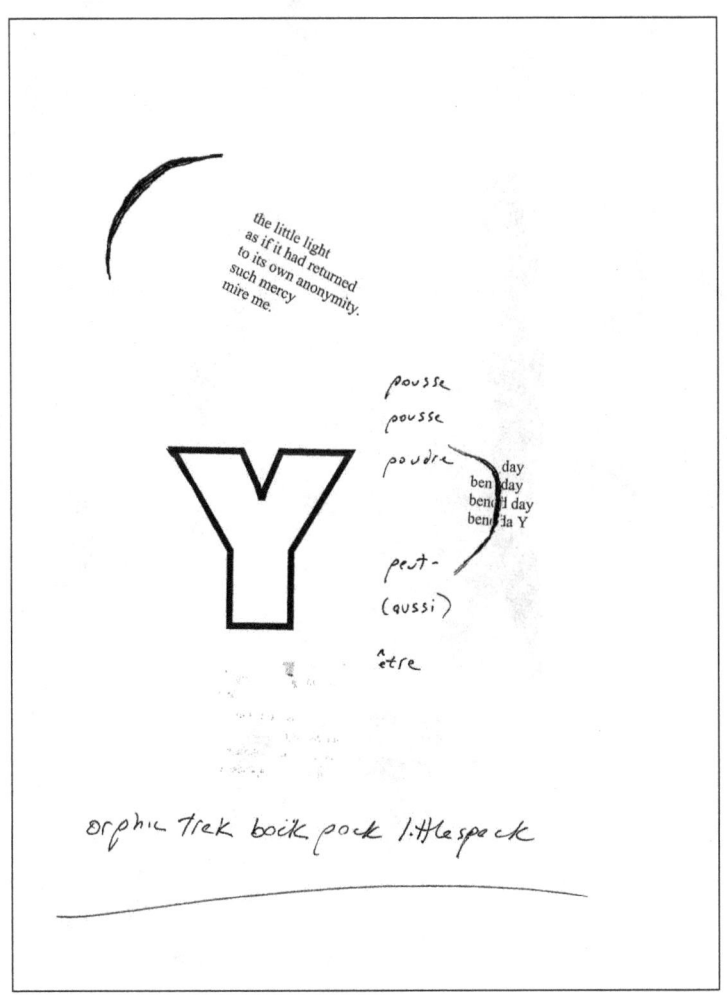

the little light
as if it had returned
to its own anonymity.
such mercy
mire me.

pousse

pousse

poudre

Y

day
ben day
ben d day
ben da Y

peut-

(aussi)

être

orphic Trek book pock littlespack

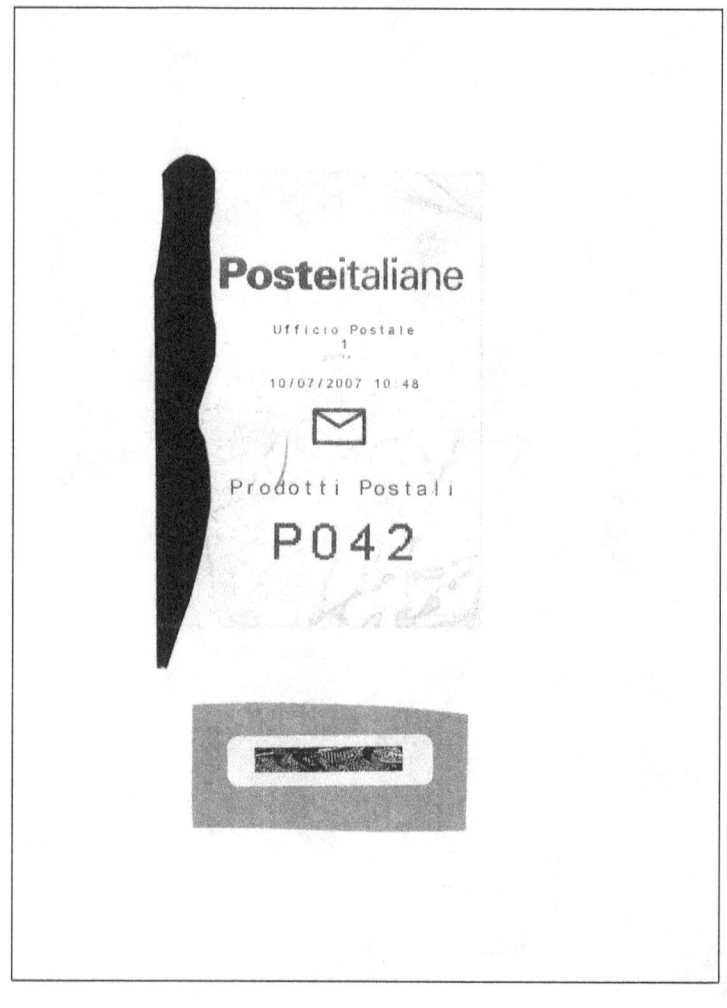

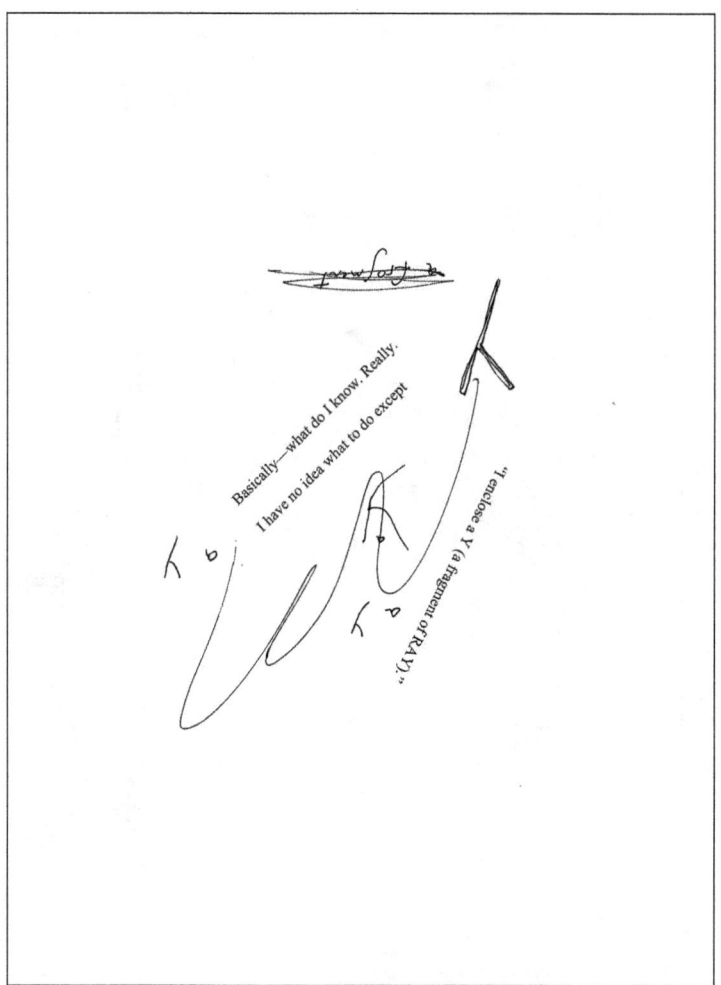

Basically—what do I know. Really.

I have no idea what to do except

"I enclose a V (a fragment of RAY)."

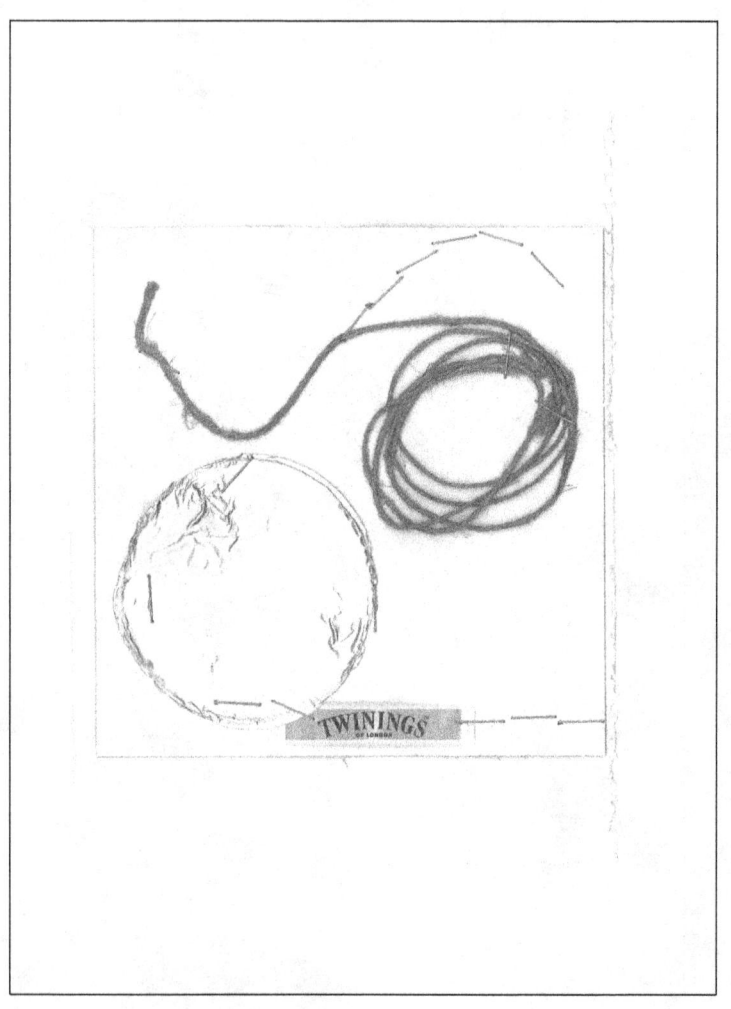

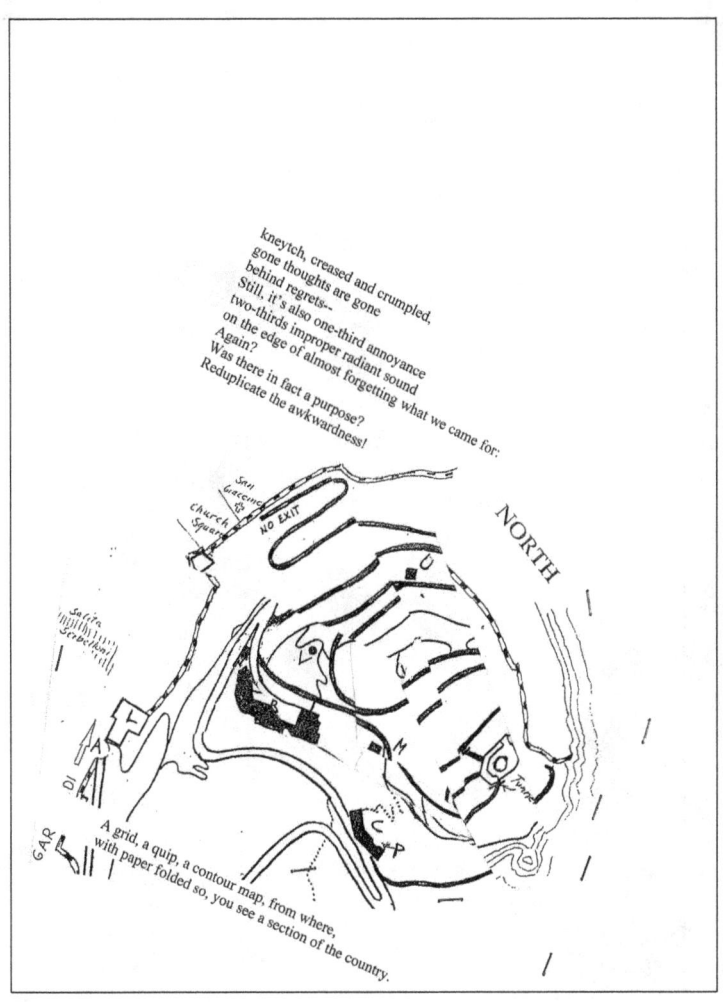

kneytch, creased and crumpled,
gone thoughts are gone
behind regrets--
Still, it's also one-third annoyance
two-thirds improper radiant sound
on the edge of almost forgetting what we came for:
Again?
Was there in fact a purpose?
Reduplicate the awkwardness!

A grid, a quip, a contour map, from where,
with paper folded so, you see a section of the country.

[159]

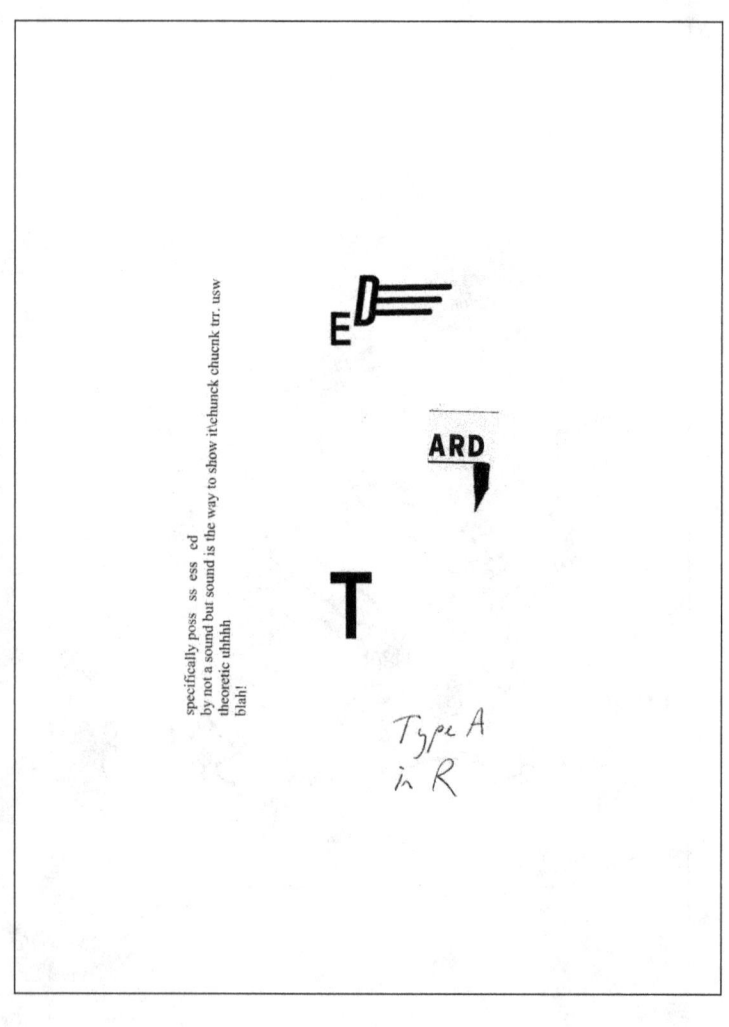

specifically poss  ss  ess  ed
by not a sound but sound is the way to show it'chunck chucnk trr. usw
theoretic uhhhh
blah!

E

ARD

T

Type A
in R

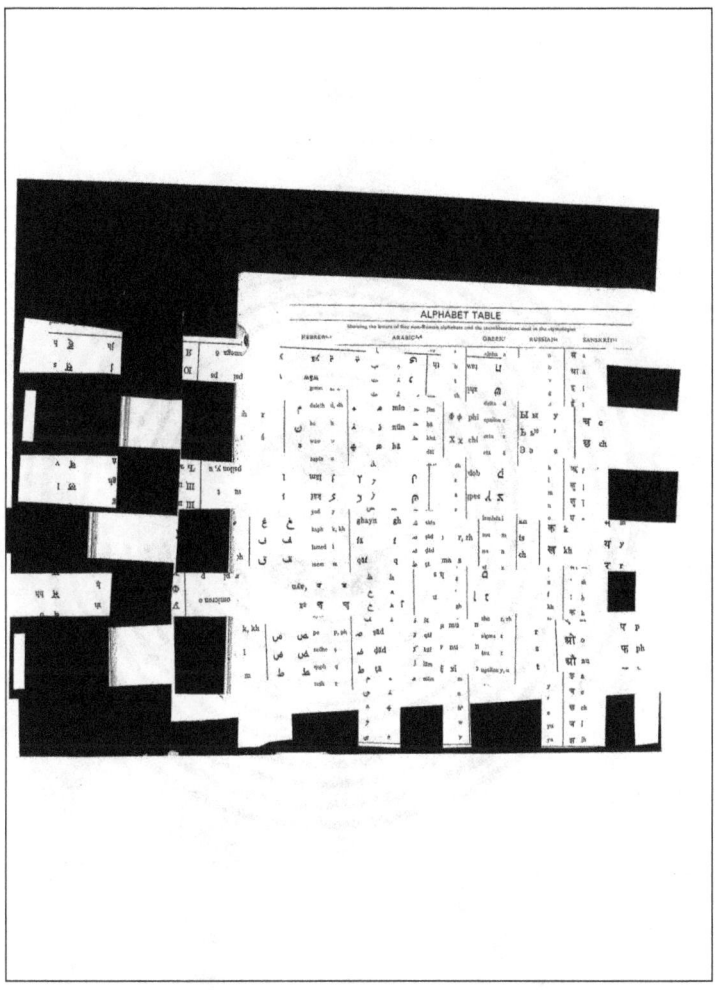

ALPHABET TABLE

Showing the letters of four non-Roman alphabets and the transliterations used in this alphabetical

swollen, tender, tendus, swilling

LA LANGUE

To want the void

within the text, yet →

---

Each single word, each labile letter
opened a mini-world
from particular presence and long implication.
it was so fast, and so distracting
and sometimes saturate with pleasure
at the exactness of calibration
in the endless vast excess.

letters flew up into the space
of codes that bring things
to face themselves not just as
themselves but as also linked
to each other and to us, in air filled with
generosity.
ferocity.

where the light is

light is centered by a small black wall
capturing air in oblique folds

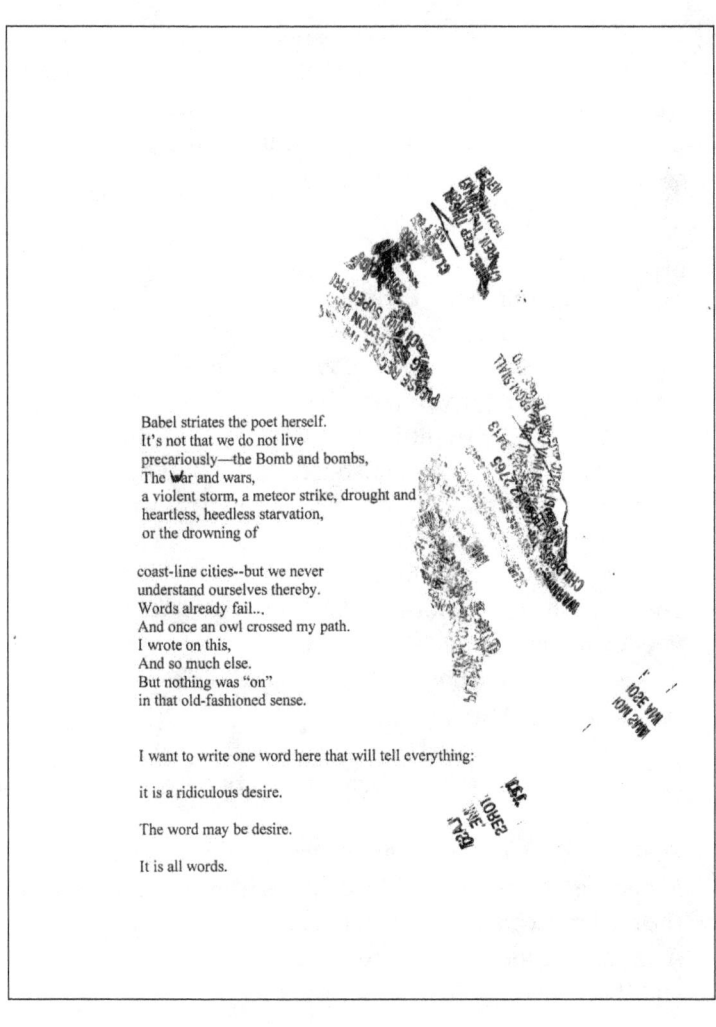

Babel striates the poet herself.
It's not that we do not live
precariously—the Bomb and bombs,
The war and wars,
a violent storm, a meteor strike, drought and
heartless, heedless starvation,
or the drowning of

coast-line cities--but we never
understand ourselves thereby.
Words already fail...
And once an owl crossed my path.
I wrote on this,
And so much else.
But nothing was "on"
in that old-fashioned sense.

I want to write one word here that will tell everything:

it is a ridiculous desire.

The word may be desire.

It is all words.

# Draft 95: Erg

An erg (symbol "erg") is the unit of energy
and mechanical work in the centimeter-
gram-second (CGS) system of units. Its name
is derived from the Greek ergon, meaning
work.

I.

Looking at a self being there
    is one, looking
        at them passing, visible, beloved and then
on a walk I don't or will not take.
    The fact, the sunlit it,
        of seeing pinkish tree
in iridescent luminosity—its pleasure mutual with mine.
    Very clunky a-syntactic lists of (ex post facto)
        words, a third.
Fourth in the ears before I fall asleep
    symphonic; orchestral intensity;
        the whoosh of music never writ
the rush and pitch
    of rhythmic blood.
        Fifth—this twisting wreath of multicolored snakes.

First, into the wind as leaves fall down. Second, mourning.
Reductive. I just said this. Third, traces. The deer, hit, explodes on
the road in blood and flesh. Explicit.
A chunk of time gets crossed with place
and this is here.

II.

R: I hold the inside out of space.
　　Just for a bit, and then it disappears.

Pen: Talk into the mini-mike
　　inside this pen.
　　　　Narrate how and why you choose.

R: It's not a bad question,
　　how do I choose, except conceptualized
　　　　sort of
like this poem, by which I mean sequentially—
　　implying scroll unrolling open.
　　　　Told like that.
No simultaneity.
　　Not recursive.
　　　　To narrate it won't work.
Decisions come instantaneously,
　　a synaptic,
　　　　evaluative insouciance
with a WTF flair, so it's
　　impossible to spell out
　　　　the how and where.

Pen: That's almost impenetrable.

R: What about a block of matter
　　presents itself so full right here,
　　　　so like an intricately textured wall

that the rest of one's life
        is soon to be spent investigating
            its in's and out's,
            in thrall to that.

Pen: I didn't think you had such a
penchant for simile.

R: Whatever's here is accident become complete
        by working it.
                It's pitching forward, as we speak.
You didn't see, but there's a lurch, you almost
        don't in time get off the bus,
                but then you did
stuck on the street, sweating, or swearing, where
        you'd almost missed that bus and
                you are panting, quite a ten block run,
but now all right, you're on.

Pen: The pentecost of every now
        breaks through the aura of what's there
                made by the ever-never was of words,
                their curls and swirls
                and limpid quivering.

R: That's right.
        (Pen: Huh?)
The intractable becomes attractive and then
        rejected; the solving for one element or an-
other on a periodic table with imaginary numbers
        gives rise to awkward balance
or unbalanced shim.
        Ergs of pulse and weight and tininess

get adjusted again and again
　　　with watch repairer's delicacy of touch.
A joule, a nano-joule
　　　a jewel of a choice, a plumpish jerk of a choice.

Pen: So forget sequence. And forget the bus.
Forget the wall. Then they are pentimentos all.

R: Now instead try vast net *worven* on side, erg
　　　　　erg, erg, with blood-Wiped woof,
warped proof
　　　debris deciding something
　　　　　amid drift and weft,
strength in the torque, aggression in the turn,
　　　momentum in the saturated gaze
　　　　　behind the everything that's here.

Someone mentioned "the murderous relation
of the elements."

Pen: It was a man you met,
depend on it; that doesn't sound like you.

R: "Murderous" (you're right, I wouldn't use),
excites me as an indication of intensities.
It's pure passion.
The head faints
inside its own
undone (un)doing
blacking out
inside the vacuum of page
emptied and full.

Pen: So are specific words expendable?

R: Absolutely not. Words stabilize
but do not deny
porosity.
It's language swooning over you and thru
    You hold it tight it's soft it's hard
        Transforms itself
      On entering you.

Pen: Taken a step further,
long poem is always an impending failure.
After all, desire's intermittent.

R: It will come again.
It's purest pleasure.
Endings, failures
are not so hidden goals along the way.
What would
"success" look like in this case?
That the patient would live?
We write Pindaric all the time
looking for victory and working as we fall, so as not
to tempt the powers that entered from the first.
We hope our heart-ribs do not burst.

Pen: This is self-serving, self-dramatizing, even
self-penalizing. And rhymed. Try something
more straight-forward like:
do you think of the reader when you write?

R: I am thinking of you, because you have intruded!
You are asking the most exacerbating questions
except for those I ask myself.

Pen: How do you link penetration and detachment?

R: I wish I could lose transcendence utterly
        (Pen: Really? What a story...)
but it is both implausible and impossible.
        (Pen: doesn't a grid suspend transcendence?)
Why not ask what I do to organize the overload?

Dream of a Pen: What are you doing here?

Dream of an R: In the real, the same.
Sometimes everything is magnetized
but not consistently.

Pen: Poignant.

R: Go away.


III.

A long black rat snake (harmless) has coiled
under that car parked along the curb
and has then to be lured
more into the open street from the gutter
and attacked by the man with a long shovel
who will hit and chop at it, and one sees its
spine and the head thrusting as it will try
to defend itself, the sadness of a snake

out of place crossed our border.

Is this what I wanted to say?
It is said. Is it what I wanted?
It is what came out.
The snake is killed.

How can I possibly indicate
what this feels like? Like having
no words

to make so many works to say
almost "without words" for
awe of it. It chose me.

> The watch I'm wearing has a quirk.
> I got it from this woman
> who is dead now.
>
> It keeps on stopping.
> It's the second hand gets caught,
> Some little flaw or piece of dirt.
>
> Whenever I see the time is wrong,
> I knock it hard to start it up again,
> hitting the table where I do my work.

NOVEMBER–DECEMBER 2008

# Notes

Notes to Draft 77: Pitch Content. Hélène Cixous, "The Book as One of Its Own Characters" is the source for the epigraph, which has been appropriated to my purposes. Cixous stated: "Books are characters in books. Between authors and books, not everything can be taken for granted ... It [the book] wants to write. It wants me to write it ..." *New Literary History* 33 (2002), 403. "The letters took on ... the shape of great mountains." Gershom Scholem, *Major Trends in Jewish Mysticism*, NY: Schocken Books [1954], 1971. The sound postulated in the universe: "Black-hole B flat" with "a period of oscillation of ten million years," as summarized by John Rockwell, *N.Y. Times* Jan. 30, 2004, E5. "Timbral extravagance," also John Rockwell, obituary for the composer Lou Harrison, Feb. 4, 2003, *N.Y. Times*. "Sideshadows" as in "Draft 32: Renga," from M.A. Bernstein and Gary Morson. "A near-traumatic astonishment": is Geoffrey Hartman about Emanuel Levinas interpreting Midrash. "Representation, Violence and the Fate of Culture: An Interview with Geoffrey Hartman," conducted by Steve Newman. *Journal of Modern Literature* 26, 3/4 (Spring 2003): 103–123. Citation from 111. This work is the fifth beginning on the "line of one."

Notes to Draft 78: Buzz Track. "Aspect-variant luminosity" (phrase from P.J. Kennelly and J.A. Kimmerling—geographers, source unremembered). Information on the European blackbird, and the collected sounds of other birds in Umbria (European gold finch, green woodpecker, blue tit, sparrow, swallow, crow, cuckoo, hoopoe) from *Collins Field Guide: Birds of Britain and Europe*. Roger Peterson, Guy Mountfort, and P.A.D. Hollom. HarperCollins, Publishers, 2004: 182, 225, 157, 208, 164, 156. Poem is on the "line of two."

Notes to Draft 79: Mass Observation. The title alludes to a social-poetic-populist writing movement begun in England in the 1930s once described as "anthropology-at-home."

"Black verse" is actually a pun by George Oppen, from the poem "Animula." "We do this by taking a long-term approach." TIAA-CREF ad, *Time*, April 24, 2006, 5. "By-the-book investigation." *International Herald Tribune*, July 1–2, 2006. "$190, 000 a day—in 2005": "On CEO Lee Ramond of ExxonMobil, now retired," *Time*, April 24, 2006, 17. "Without the fat & calories": ad, *Time*, April 24, 2006, 70. "There will be much to avoid in this poem": Robert Southey on *Thalaba* apparently; I don't know where. "Outcry about mistaken policies," (also cited in Draft 47) from *International Herald Tribune*, August 3, 2001. The "5-passenger sanctuary from the worst the elements can throw at you": Toyota ad in *Time*, April 24, 2006, 1. Questions about close-ups and long shots, in a symposium at the Umbria Film Festival, July 8, 2006, asked by Lone Scherfig, the Danish film director. Poem is on the "line of three."

Notes to Draft 80: Envoi. "Striking combinations of organic and inorganic elements, contaminating conventional artistic structures with rebellious uses of unconventional objects." Cheim & Read Gallery brochure on the work of Jannis Kounellis. Poem is on the "line of four."

Notes to Draft 82: Hinge. "We stand bewildered . . ." is a citation of Rilke's argument, made just after the beginning of World War I, that art and theater should have prevented that war. The Rilke material (in a letter from June 1915) is discussed in George Rochberg, *The Aesthetics of Survival: A Composer's View of Twentieth-Century Music*. William Bolcom, ed. Ann Arbor: University of Michigan Press, 1984, 219. "See, I have inscribed you on the palms of my hands" is the actual citation from Isaiah 49: 16, modified here. Poem is on the "line of six."

Notes to Draft 83: Listings. Some of the "media" in which people work are taken from the handout written by Phyllis Rosenzweig, for "Zero to Infinity: Arte Povera, 1962–1972." Smithsonian Museum, The Hirshhorn Museum and Sculpture Garden, 2002. Basket making language from a brochure from an exhibit from the Hudson Museum: Tree & Tradition, Brown Ash and Maine Native American Basket Making. Exhibit seen October 1995–96 at the Maine Center for the Arts, University of Maine at Orono. The lead books are by Anselm Kiefer, an installation at the Hamburger Bahnhof Museum, Berlin. More of his lead library was seen at the Grand Palais, Paris, June 2007. Poem is on the "line of seven."

Notes to Draft 84: Juncture. The cookbook is the *Joy of Cooking*. Edited by Irma S. Rombauer with later editions adding Marion Rombauer Becker, it has been in print continuously since 1936. The line "The reminds me of every/ thing." from Eileen Myles, *Sorry, Tree*; Seattle: Wave Books, 2007. The title "Taking an Interest in Clouds and Haze," from catalogue number 143, *Ike Taiga and Tokoyama Gyokuran: Japanese Masters of the Brush* (on loan from the Eisei Bunko Museum, Tokyo), show at the Philadelphia Museum of Art, 2007. Poem is on the "line of eight."

Notes to Draft 85: Hard Copy. This poem, as will be evident, is mapped loosely on, thinks about, and responds to George Oppen's 1968 work "Of Being Numerous." This includes citations both marked as quotations (as in sections 4, 9 and 40) and unmarked (as in sections 10 and 18), allusions, and variations around keywords in Oppen's sections.

The epigraph from Paul Celan, "The Meridian"; Speech on the occasion of receiving the Georg Büchner Prize, Darmstadt, October 22, 1960, translated by Rosmarie Waldrop. In *Paul Celan, Selections*, ed. Pierre Joris. Berkeley: University of California Press, 2005.

The stanza "with what is under the surface trying to come to light" is cited and modified from a brochure for the A.I.R. Gallery written by Lucy Lippard, 1976. The citation at the end of section 1 is Walter Benjamin, "Surrealism: The Last Snapshot of the European Intelligentsia" (1929), translated by Rodney Livingstone. In *Selected Writings, Volume 2, 1927–34*, ed. Michael W. Jennings. Cambridge, Mass.: The Belknap Press of Harvard University, 1999, 216 (inclusive pages 206–224). The word "apocalyptic" in section 6 draws on Robin Blaser's argument that the scale of the lyric is precisely anti-apocalyptic, in *The Fire: Collected Essays of Robin Blaser*, ed. Miriam Nichols. Berkeley: University of California Press, 2006, 93, 97. In section 8, the Legion of Honor medal alludes to Maurice Papon. Convicted of crimes against humanity in 1998 for his part in the transport of Jews from France to their deaths in Nazi concentration camps, he was no longer allowed to wear the medal, awarded to him by Charles de Gaulle for service to the country during the Algerian War—a service also marked by political thuggery and murder. When he died in February 2007, his lawyer, Francis Vuillemin said "I will personally ensure that he will be accompanied in his grave by the order of the Commander of the Legion of Honor, which he received from the hands of Charles de Gaulle, for eternity." *International Herald Tribune*, Monday, February 19, 2007, on the front page and p. 3. In section 10, "Children picking up pieces of the dead . . ." is from the *International Herald Tribune*, Wednesday, February 14, 2007, p. 5, under the headline "Iraq to Seal Borders for Baghdad Security," from AP news and IHT. In section 15, "felt-and-fat-and-dirt-and-muslin-maze" comes from a sympathetic comment by John R. Keene in his blog J's Theater, describing my work in *Drafts: http://www.inblogs.net/jstheater/2005/05* from Tuesday, May 24, 2005. In section 21, there is a glancing allusion to Wislawa Szymborska's poem "May be left untitled," from *People on a Bridge*, trans. Adam Czerniawski. London: Forest Books, 1996, 56–57. In section 25, the description of the isolated double basses, from James Freeman, program notes (slightly modified), for Arthur Honegger's *Symphony No. 2 for String Orchestra and Trumpet* (1941); program from concert, Orchestra 2001, January 29, 1995. The citation in section 26 is from Meredith Quartermain's response to an earlier version of this poem. Section 33 is first based on an insight by Juliana Spahr in *thisconnectionofeveryonewithlungs: Poems*, Berkeley: University of California Press, 2005, and finishes with the end of a citation from R.W. Emerson: "Crossing a bare common in snow puddles at twilight, under a clouded sky . . . glad to the brink of fear" from "Nature." In section 34, thanks to Drury Sherrod. One poet alluded to is Rilke, in *Duino Elegies*. The citation in section 35 from Ann Snitow, in conversation. The material cited in section 37 comes from my first book, *Wells* (1980). Poem is on the "line of nine." It was begun at Bellagio, with much gratitude for that residency.

Notes to Draft 86: Scarpbook. "Scarpbook" is Ray Johnson's typo for scrapbook; see William S. Wilson, "Ray Johnson: The One and the Other," in Donna De Salvo and Catherine Gudis, eds. *Ray Johnson:*

*Correspondences*. Columbus, Ohio: Wexner Center for the Arts, 1999: 165–175. This poem was written in some measure to participate in a New Zealand-Italy conjuncture instigated by Michele Leggott for the New Zealand Studies Association conference held in Florence in summer 2008. "Villa d'Este  Staten Island" was the title of a poem of mine from the early 1960s and is also the source of the line "fountains, stairways, ferries, and polychrome money." "Train journey and journey by water" is the first line of another poem from the 1960s that was recuperated into my first book, *Wells* (1980). The line "a fire-bed of 48 extinct volcanos," the overlook called Maungawhau (Mt. Eden), and a sense of Rangitoto as given by Michele Leggott, describing elements of Auckland about which I inquired for this poem. "Theory is gray, but life is green." James Smethurst, in a reader's report; little did I know then that this might be taken to allude to Zukofsky's "A"–8, 53. "The data set in vector format" is a phrase by John Sorrentino. "Incoherent tunneling," is a phrase by Peter Riseborough. "Earth has not anything to show more fair" is the first line of Wordsworth's Westminster Bridge sonnet. The coordinates of the relevant cities are Firenze 43 47 N and 11 15 E; Auckland 36 52 S; and 174 46 E; Philadelphia 39 57 N and 75 10 W. Poem is on the "line of ten."

Notes to Draft 87: Trace Elements. This poem was conceptualized for and delivered as a plenary address at a conference called Poetics of the Trace, held at Monash University, Melbourne, Australia in July 2008. After I finished this poem, I re-found the following citation used in *Blue Studios*; it speaks to one project of this poem. "'J-F Lyotard makes the unrepresentable what all representation must strive to represent and what it must also be aware of not being able to represent; he makes the forgotten what all memory must strive to remember but what it cannot remember.'" This is from the foreword by David Carroll to Jean-François Lyotard, *Heidegger and 'the jews'* (1988), Trans. Andreas Michel and Mark S. Roberts. Minneapolis: University of Minnesota Press, 1990, xiii. Further, trace being, among other possibilities, a Derridean concept, at least one of the workings of trace in this poem is generally indebted to Niall Lucy, *A Derrida Dictionary*. Oxford: Blackwell Publishing, 2004 and to Leslie Hill, *The Cambridge Introduction to Jacques Derrida*. Cambridge University Press, 2007. Trace being also a very important concept for studies of the psychology of memory and for the philosophy of memory, this poem, when partly written, was given an important jolt by John Sutton, "Memory," *The Stanford Encyclopedia of Philosophy* (Summer 2004 Edition), Edward N. Zalta (ed.) *http://plato.stanford.edu/archives/sum2004/entries/memory/* Accessed April 20, 2008. Several syntactically altered citations and one central concept from Sutton are used in this poem. Sutton is the source of the citation "each memory is many memories," as well as the nearby list based on his words: "Outside philosophy and the courtroom, perhaps we only recognise human memory as operating 'normally' when its successes are shot through with instances of forgetting, selection, condensation, interference, and distortion." The little posi-

tivist reminders about evaluating research protocols were found acci-
dentally, on the back of some scrap paper I picked up in my workplace.
I don't, therefore, know their source. Reference to the Trace is to the
Natchez Trace. The citation ("every photograph is an archive: from the
moment of its inception, it records the past—or, at least, a glimpse of
it"), Susie Linfield, "Every Photo an Archive," *The Nation* 286. 17 (May 5,
2008): 30–33. Citation from 31. "My life takes time," citation from
"Section IV: Going Away" of a work by Anne Tardos called "The Aim of
All Nature Is Beauty," in *Critiphoria www.critiphoria.org/issue1/
Anne_Tardos.pdf* Accessed May 2, 2008. The "compact hyperbolic surface"
is appropriated language from the Selberg trace formula—a subfield of
mathematics. Mathematics uses a concept of the trace that was brought
into this poem verbally without my having one single clue as to what
this language means in its actual context. The quotation that begins "A
visible mark or sign . . ." is the first definition of "trace" in the *American
Heritage Dictionary*. The statement "So I went back trying to find a trace of
what had been there" is cited from Jerome Rothenberg's explanation
about his works concerning Poland and Shoah during his poetry reading
on April 28, 2008 at Kelly Writers House, Philadelphia. The material
about the mini-solar system is from an article by Dennis Overbye in the
*New York Times*, February 15, 2008. Headline: "Smaller Version of the Solar
System Is Discovered." The first sentences are: "Astronomers have found
a miniature version of our own solar system 5,000 light years across the
galaxy — the first planetary system that really looks like our own. The
discovery, they said, means that our solar system may be more typical of
planetary systems across the universe than had been thought." In the
article, astronomer Sara Seager is cited as stating: "right now in exoplan-
ets we are on an inexorable path to finding other Earths." The acronym
TRACE does mean Transition Region and Coronal Explorer—a small
mission launched by NASA on April 2, 1998; it is a space telescope
providing high-resolution images of the sun's phenomena, including
coronal loops. "'To unexpress the expressible'"; "inexprimer l'ex-
primable." These citations are from Roland Barthes, in Jonathan Culler,
*Barthes: A Very Short Introduction*. Oxford UP, 2002, 129. Barthes' citations
from *Le Bruissement de la langue*; in English as *The Rustle of Language*, tr.
Richard Howard, Hill and Wang, 1986, xvii. "Nothing beside remains . . ."
from the poem "Ozymandias" by P.B. Shelley. The technique of kintsugi,
seen in the exhibit "The Collections of Barbara Bloom" (International
Center of Photography, NYC, Spring 2008), uses gold-filled lacquer to
repair ceramics in order to "illuminate the breakage"; this citation from
the *New Yorker* paragraph on the show, March 3, 2008, 11. "The excess of
the word refuses to forget" is from Michum Huehls on Harryette Mullen.
"Spun Puns (and Anagrams): Exchange Economies, Subjectivity and
History in Harryette Mullen's *Muse & Drudge*." *Contemporary Literature* 44.
1 (Spring 2003): 19–46. "Fine porcelain and some stunning factory
seconds": from an article in the *Philadelphia Inquirer*, Wed., April 2, 2008.
D5, by-line Stephan Salisbury. "She" is Alexandra Alevizatos Kirtley, cura-
tor of an exhibit at the Philadelphia Museum on Bonnin and Morris,

colonial Philadelphia porcelain, coincidentally going on at the time that shards including Bonnin and Morris ceramics were discovered in South Philly. The word "mongo," found in an article in the *New York Times* is apparently used by trash collectors in NYC to indicate useable objects recuperated from the trash. A related word seems to be "mungo": reclaimed wool used for cheap cloth. "There are no truly green stars." *National Audubon Society Field Guide to the Night Sky*. NY: Knopf, 1991, don't know the page number now. "My hand goes down on the page. I etch means of portage, marks of debris, failures of infrastructure. I rip these images out of the newspaper" is cited from Amze Emmons, informal artist's talk at the Print Club of Philadelphia, March 15, 2008. Ralph Waldo Emerson, "History" is the source of the lines "Who knows this or that?/ Hark in the wall to the rat." From *Collected Poems and Translations*. NY: Library of America, 1994, 385. A very suggestive article by Jessica Dubow, "Case Interrupted: Benjamin and the Dialectical Image." *Critical Inquiry* 33 (Summer 2007): 820–836 became the source for several citations. The citation "Theory is made modest and provisional . . ." comes from 825. "Crushed, inconspicuous, neglected" is cited from Patrick Pritchett (on Oppen and Palmer) who is himself citing Peter Dews (*http://jacketmagazine.com/36/oppen-pritchett.shtml*) Description of the Purple Hair-streak from Tom Tolman, *Collins Field Guide to Butterflies of Britain and Europe*. Harper Collins, 1997, 19. Being concerned with investigation suggested by Tzvetan Todorov, from an article called "The Typology of Detective Fiction." As for The Imaginary Museum of the Sardine. I have the little pamphlet in my possession. Its address is Association Ichtus, 2, rue Alsace-Loraine, 34200 Sete, France. The brochure states: «Nous connaissons tous la sardine pour y avoir goûté. La sardine est universelle. On la trouve dans toutes les mers du globe et, en boîte, elle s'est répandue sur toute la planète. Aussi, en l'isolant comme valeur emblématique de notre époque, le Musée Imaginaire de la Sardine se propose de démontrer le role fondamental de la sardine dans notre univers mental . . .» "How to tolerate an inconsolable instant . . ." again from Jessica Dubow, "Case Interrupted: Benjamin and the Dialectical Image." This citation from 834. "Crossed products with continuous trace" is the title of a book in mathematical theory by Siegfried Echterhoff, published in 1996 by the American Mathematical Society. "A fleeting but sharp pulsation of historical awareness" is from Todd Carmody, "The Banality of the Document: Charles Reznikoff's *Holocaust* and Ineloquent Empathy," *jml* (32.1). The loss of the pages (and, of course, the records) from several 16th and 17th century archival folders occurred in Tourcoing, France; the story that they were indeed used to wrap *frites* is attested by the then-archivist, as told to Robert DuPlessis. "The fragment is an indispensable thought form . . . where the break occurs— where the fragment breaks" . . . from Marjorie Welish, "Contemplating Table(t)s. Review of Norma Cole," *Jacket* 31 (October 2006). *http://jacketmagazine.com/31/welish-cole.html* "The intemperate presence of the micro"-substance, again Jessica Dubow, as above *Critical Inquiry* 33 (Spring 2007), 823. The dotted paintings leading to water are an allusion to the map, mythic, and title deed functions of Australian aboriginal art. Learning "to read the book within the book," Edmund Jabès, "The Key," in *Midrash and Literature*, eds. Geoffrey Hartmann and Sanford Budick, Yale UP, 1986, 352. There is an allusion, at the end, to Simon Rodia's Watts Towers in a neighborhood of Los Angeles. John Sutton's encyclopedia article on memory, url above, ends with a discussion of current theories that posit memory as in part "external" and configured socially and culturally as a feedback system in relation to individual memory. This is the concept of "dynamical cognition" that he describes as a threefold "embodied, embedded, and extended mind." It was startling to have a confluence between one aspect of this poem's findings: a sense of poetry's importance as "embodied, embedded, and extended mind" (citation from Sutton), even in the form of evanescent traces, and the argument offered by this philosopher of psychology for a social as well as personal memory, a social memory sometimes found in cultural artifacts. The pertinent list of social cues is also derived/cited from Sutton: "the various kinds of memory scaffolding which humans use, from knots, rhymes, codes, diagrams, slide-rules, and sketch pads to artificial memory techniques, photographs, books, rituals, and computers, have quite different properties, so that the resources of the historian, media theorist, and social scientist may again have a role within cognitive science." It could be appropriate to append "poet" to this list as helping to investigate these properties. Poem is on the "line of eleven."

Notes to Draft 88: X-Posting. This Draft is based on Ingeborg Bachmann's important poem "Keine Delikatessen." The parts directly using her words are in italics here. In this poem, she wonders about the adequacy of poetry and of her poetry. Finding this poem—needing it and looking for it—I then began trans-interpreting it, transposing it, elaborating, extending, varying it, working homophonically with the German, and creating my variation of it by writing a poem that started with hers and that in large measure tracks her argument in a free variation on Bachmann. I would like to thank Marion Faber for her courtesy in sending me a translation when I was without library resources. Mark Anderson's translation is from *In the Storm of Roses: Selected Poems by Ingeborg Bachmann*. Princeton: Princeton University Press, 1986, 186–189. While working on this poem, I also received commentary from the poet Anne Blonstein, whose queries, sympathy with Bachmann's text, and help with certain moments of the German were of great importance to what I have done. Although this is now hardly a translation, if I am in any sense "translating" Bachmann's poem, this occurs only along the lines that Walter Benjamin suggests when he says: "as regards the meaning, the language of a translation can—in fact, must—let itself go, so that it gives voice to the *intentio* of the original not as reproduction but as harmony, as a supplement to the language in which it expresses itself, as its own kind of *intentio*." ("The Task of the Translator," *Illuminations*, 78–79). Poem is on the "line of twelve."

Notes to Draft 89: Interrogation. This poem was occasioned most directly by the writing of "Draft 88: X-Posting," varying a poem by Ingeborg Bachmann. "Death is the mother of beauty," is from Wallace Stevens, "Sunday Morning." There is a citation from Bob Perelman: "The whole/ language to/ unlearn." *IFLIFE*, NY: Roof Books, 2006, 25. The final line, "I still haven't been able to figure out what happened here," is by Samuel R. Delany, *Dhalgren* [1974]. NY: Vintage Books, 2001, 459. Poem is on the "line of thirteen."

Notes to Draft XC: Excess. The arresting question "What is this that wants this?" is cited from Bob Grenier, *Attention*. This pamphlet for the "Curriculum of the Soul" series was accessed on the Eclipse website. This citation is on 25. "The excess of the word refuses to forget" is the actual citation from Michum Huehls on Harryette Mullen, see Draft 87: Trace Elements. Poem is on the "line of fourteen."

Notes to Draft 91: Proverbs. The upside down Capitol is a motif in Theodore Harris's collages. Poem is on the "line of fifteen."

Notes to Draft 92: Translocation. One of the generators for this poem's interest in one's own foreignness of time, place, and language was taking the poem "This Lime Tree Bower, My Prison" by S.T. Coleridge and running the English through Google translation programs into French, then German, then back to English. Some of that language is used (and modified). One line of the poem comes from student Kari Barlow. There is a comment on Michael O'Brien's "Those Days," *Sleeping and Waking*. Some of the language is taken and modified from short reports by Parker Shipton and Nancy Maclean about their projects at the National Humanities Center. The poem is beholden in general to Durham, North Carolina. Poem is on the "line of sixteen."

Notes for Draft 94: Mail Art (a black and white selection). The visual in "Official Photo" is the hairball advertising the *International Herald Tribune*, appearing in Sat–Sun. Feb 3, 2007, on 5. The page beginning "The predominance of lines was an international . . ." has several sources to credit. Anita Haldemann wrote the art historical text, from her brochure for the exposition "Neoclassicism to Early Modernism, Positions of Drawing in the 19th Century," Kunstmuseum Basel in the Kupferstichkabinett. The composer Junghae Lee wrote the text in German as a description of her "Sonorletten fur Kalviertrio mit Elektronik (2006)" heard at Gare du Nord concert space, in Basel. The French comes from a brochure from the Beyeler Museum in Basel. All Basel materials are indebted to the hospitality of Anne Blonstein. "Shivering as heavy rains" uses the alphabet table from *Webster's Ninth New Collegiate Dictionary*. Springfield, MA: Merriam-Webster, Inc., 1986, 74. The Hebrew text is cited/photocopied from *The Burnt Book: Reading the Talmud* by Marc-Alan Ouaknin, trans. Llewellyn Brown, Princeton: Princeton University Press, 1995, 110–111. The page "Basically—what do

I know" cites "I enclose a Y . . ." from Ray Johnson, *The Paper Snake*. New York: Something Else Press, 1965, n.p.

The weaving uses the alphabet table from *Webster's Ninth New Collegiate Dictionary*. Springfield, MA: Merriam-Webster, Inc., 1986, 74. The definitions of tongue, of LA LANGUE are from *Webster's Ninth New Collegiate Dictionary*. Springfield, MA: Merriam-Webster, Inc., 1986, 1242.

Notes to Draft 95: Erg. The epigraph is from Wikipedia. The poem was provoked by a letter from a stranger, Shaleigh Kwok, a graduate student in psychology at Temple University, with a research question. The man whom I cite is probably Simon Jarvis, from a conference paper. Poem is on the "line of 19."